With an engaging and entertaining presentation style, Marli's MIRROR Method offers managers and leaders practical and insightful solutions to addressing even the most challenging dysfunctional workplace behaviors. Her approach has proven to be applicable to almost any workplace challenge and, thus far, has produced significant improvements in the workplace culture and the confidence of the leaders to manage dysfunctional behavior.

– **Jason Giesbrecht,** Chief Operating Officer, Golden Life Management

Marli Rusen is in a category unto herself! She is a credible and captivating facilitator/guest speaker! Marli brings a wealth of lived experience and expertise that she translates into stories and "lessons" which resonate with her participants. Her methods and tools are practical, relevant, straightforward and easily understood. Her MIRROR Method offers a realistic, step-by-step approach that can be applied across a broad spectrum of leadership/management activities.

Marli's "quirky" sense of humor quickly engages her "audience;" her quick wit combined with her direct, no-nonsense delivery is extremely effective at getting the message across. She has a masterful gift for getting participants to see – and sometimes ruefully laugh at – themselves in her examples and stories. People come away from Marli's sessions feeling empowered, enlightened, invigorated and positive. They have a clearer understanding of their responsibilities and greater confidence and competence in their ability to carry them out.

As you can tell, I am a huge Marli Rusen fan and have tremendous respect for her work! She is "one in a million" and I have no hesitation in recommending her to any organization!

– **Barbara J. (Barb) Severyn,** Executive Director, Human Resources, Camosun College

Our organization has engaged Marli to conduct environmental scans as well as investigations and to deliver her education series, The MIRROR Method. Marli's insightful, practical approach to assess dysfunction and bring the right tools and recommendations to address it has allowed the organization to take action to both resolve specific situations and to provide organizational learnings by identifying systemic issues and barriers. Marli is an amazing facilitator who delivers information in a highly engaging, accessible, and humorous manner. I highly recommend

Marli as an educator and investigator and look forward to any future opportunities to work with Marli.

– **Patricia J Devlin,** Specialist, Respectful Workplace, Island Health

Marli has been working with BC Nurses' Union over the past year with the goal of ensuring our internal policies and procedures are in line with new legislation aimed at preventing harassment and bullying in the workplace. Marli was also asked to develop and deliver workshops for our frontline staff with the intention of providing practical advice on steps they can take to reduce dysfunctional conflict at our workplace. A separate workshop was designed and delivered for our leadership team with the aim of providing them the tools needed to detect and manage disrespectful conduct. All of Marli's sessions were customized to meet the uniqueness of our workplace.

As the organizer of Marli's staff and leadership workshops, I had the pleasure of hosting and attending one of the scheduled events. I can tell you without hesitation that Marli is a skilled, charismatic presenter with a natural talent of engaging and capturing her audiences' interest. She has a relaxed instructional approach that uses a combination of direct and indirect elements. She uses appropriate humor to create a relaxed, interactive learning environment and her use of case studies created opportunities for learner involvement. Marli was able to manage situations with ease when her content was being challenged by learners and did so without affecting the flow of the workshop. I not only experienced all of these qualities in the event I attended but this was also consistent with other sessions as evidenced through formal workshop evaluations.

In addition to the many positive written evaluations, I had a number of staff tell me that they valued and related to the material Marli presented and that they felt better equipped to handle situations in the future. I even had one of our leaders tell me about using the tools immediately after taking the training and felt empowered by taking the steps Marli presented in her training when addressing a situation that arose. When surveyed, over 90% of staff agreed or strongly agreed that the material presented was relevant and that they felt confident applying what they learned in the workplace.

– **Colleen McFadden,** CHRP, EMBA Sr. Director, Human Resources & Operations, BC Nurses' Union

Marli Rusen is a king maker and a bricklayer to most castles, though she never stays long enough to enjoy the sweat and tears of her hard work. I experienced Marli's impeccable reputation in the past 4 years ... Marli's high level of facilitation and leadership is sprinkled with her attractive personality that illustrates a grand sense of humor, integrity, trustworthiness, humility and wisdom and varied lived experiences.

I always say if you are not ready to act do not engage Marli. She brings a true mirror to your leadership as a manager, director or CEO. What you see in the mirror is who you are in how you lead yourself and/or others. Marli is the best Mirror every leader needs throughout their leadership journey. Those accessing Marli's skills and publications will be fortunate and augmented. Enjoy!

– Francis Garwe, B.Sc., MAOM-HCM, CCM, CMP, Director, Clinical Services, Durham Community Health Centre

A well respected, delightful presenter, who is able to discuss challenging issues using clear and understandable language, we have used Marli's expertise quite extensively over the past several years. Marli's wisdom, varied life experiences and sense of humor are just a few of the strengths she brings to bear, using the principles of *The Mirror Method* to support and guide leaders with their approach to developing teams. This book is a must for any organization looking to make a difference.

– David Williams, MBA, CHRP, Vice President, Human Resources, Northern Health

As an employment lawyer who frequently deals with dysfunctional workplaces on behalf of employees, unions and employers, I have always respected Marli Rusen's insightful and effective work in resolving workplace conflict. At a time when employers face increasing scrutiny for how they address inappropriate conduct, Marli's proactive approach is a welcome salve for the issues that create the modern toxic workplace. *The MIRROR Method* is a model for how leaders can do the difficult work of creating kindness in the workplace and ensuring that all employees are treated fairly and respectfully.

– Peter Eastwood, Lawyer, Vancouver BC

The
MIRROR METHOD

How to build productive teams by
ending workplace dysfunction

MARLI RUSEN

Brilliant Idea Books

This work has been carefully researched and verified for accuracy; however, due to the complexity of the subject matter and the continual changes occurring in the subject matter, the author cannot be held responsible for errors or omissions, or consequences of any actions resulting from information in this book. Examples discussed are intended as general guidelines only. Fictional names and characters bearing any resemblance to real persons or events are purely coincidental.

ISBN (Paperback): 978-0-9938387-4-3
ISBN (e-Book): 987·0-9938387-6-7

Library and Archives Canada Cataloguing in Publication

Rusen, Marli, author

> The mirror method : how to build productive teams
> by ending workplace dysfunction / Marli Rusen.

ISBN 978-0-9938387-4-3 (hardback)

1. Organizational behavior. 2. Interpersonal relations.
3. Teams in the workplace. I. Title.

HD58.7.R88 2016   658.3   C2016-905349-0

First Printing

Publishing Consultant: **Brilliant Idea Books**
Editor: **Catherine Leek for Green Onion Publishing**
Cover and interior design, electronic page composition:
>   **Kim Monteforte for WeMakeBooks.ca**
Figure designer: **Darren Warner for Ideation + Persuasion**

Printed and bound in Canada

CONTENTS

Step 4: **Designing and Implementing Individual Remedies**   167

Step 5: **Operational Restoration: Remedying Team Dysfunction**   183

Step 6: **Revisiting the Scene of the Dysfunction**   191

Workplace Dysfunction Is Costing You a Fortune!

- The opinionated and overbearing colleague or leader who shuts others down
- The coworker who freezes others out with her heavy sighs, weighted silence and icy stares
- The micro-managing, hypervigilant manager who allows no room for feedback, input, creativity or autonomy
- The moody, unpredictable coworker around whom others walk on eggshells
- The angry and threatening CEO
- The gossiping, manipulative, passive-aggressive team member who stirs up the drama and then goes into hiding

These individuals eat up significant time, energy and profits in workplaces everywhere. They ruin the health of others – and the overall organization – because no one is stopping them from doing so.

A review of the daily court rosters, front page news and judicial decisions highlights the prevalence of these disruptive, dysfunctional behaviors in the modern workplace and their significant costs to both the organizations in which they take place and – perhaps more significantly – the valued individuals at whom they are directed.

Workplace dysfunction – in its various manifestations – is eating away at the health, profitability and productivity of individuals and workplaces everywhere.

It knows no bounds and is limitless in its application. It shows up in hospitals, at construction sites, in educational and financial institutions, lunchrooms, restrooms and executive boardrooms. It infiltrates public and private sector organizations. It seeps into non-profit societies, volunteer organizations and multi-million-dollar enterprises.

Disruptive and disrespectful behavior is not associated with or limited to a particular gender, age, profession, educational level, industry, country or cultural background.

The financial costs associated with this behavior are substantial. Dysfunctional workplaces are associated with significant absenteeism, high turnover and challenging recruitment issues, low morale, reduced productivity, intolerable error rates and a systemic lack of engagement.

So why does it exist? For one simple reason: because workplace leaders have tolerated it, excused it, ignored it, justified it and, at times, participated in it directly.

As the behavior festers and worsens over time, valuable employees leave. The "stars" on the team go elsewhere, taking their expertise with them. Those broken from the dysfunction are forced to take medical leaves. Many file complex lawsuits/complaints focused on their work environments and the unmanaged behavior of others. Most share their experience with others, including colleagues, competitors and, increasingly, journalists hungry for the "scoop" on high profile workplace drama and dysfunction, particularly when it involves the actions or inaction of powerful, influential leaders.

There has been increased cultural and legal recognition of the personal, professional and institutional damage associated with persistent and unacceptable workplace behaviors. In numerous jurisdictions, there are workplace policies, procedures and regulations prohibiting systemic disrespect, harassment and bullying. Leaders at every level of organizations are now expected to build and maintain respectful workplaces through controlling their own behavior and addressing the inappropriate conduct of others. The lack of timely and proper accountability for unacceptable workplace behavior has resulted in costly awards against companies and serious scrutiny of the leadership involved.

Separate and apart from the legal consequences, the human carnage arising from systemic inaction in the face of inappropriate behavior is evident in workplaces everywhere. People lose sleep, become sick, get divorced and often lose their jobs (commonly, ones they love) because of dysfunctional team members or management with whom they are forced to work.

For this dysfunction to end, workplaces must commit to cultivating genuine environments of respect and professionalism. For this to happen, all leaders – from frontline supervisors to CEOs – must stop excusing the inexcusable (in themselves and others) and start taking action.

There is no evidence-based reason to allow this behavior to continue. Intuitively we know this.

Why then does it continue? For two key reasons.

First, far too often, those in leadership are told they can't or shouldn't act; the person is too important, brings in too much money or files too many lawsuits. It will be too costly, they say, not realizing the magnified costs of inaction. The lack of institutional courage to take on dysfunctional conduct and hold individuals accountable is a significant impediment to building respectful and productive workplaces.

Second, even when leaders are permitted to act, they are not given the necessary education, tools or supports to do so in a fair, respectful and defensible manner. That is, they are told they *can* take action – but often are never shown *how*.

The MIRROR Method provides solutions to both of these issues. First, it explains why leaders must hold individuals accountable for their unacceptable conduct and performance; and then shows leaders how to do so. It is a practical framework – for leaders everywhere – on how to effectively detect, diagnose and deal with dysfunction in a defensible manner.

The first half of the book will provide leaders with a better understanding of the term "dysfunction" and what it means to have a "dysfunctional team" or "dysfunctional team member," based on modern-day expectations surrounding appropriate workplace behavior – professionally, legally and practically. This is critical because leaders need to know "what" to address before addressing it.

The second half of the book provides leaders with a straightforward six-step process to apply to any type of apparent workplace dysfunction, stemming from rude/disruptive behavior, interpersonal conflicts, bullying, persistently poor performance, paralyzing perfectionism, caustic cliques/ camps, personal, racial or sexual harassment or otherwise.

The MIRROR Method helps leaders unpack and understand complex workplace dynamics using a straightforward and defensible, evidence-based process. In applying this process, leaders will be able to determine what is truly happening on their team and – most importantly – how to address it in a timely, substantive and lasting manner.

Why Every Leader Needs the MIRROR Method

Recently, a CEO of a technology company said, "I don't need a book. I don't need a method. I just hire smart and fire fast."

This position fails to capture the complexities of dysfunction and disrespect and the financial and legal implications that flow from fast and often premature decisions to terminate those who are viewed as "problem people."

First, some dysfunctional and disruptive team members are strong performers who provide significant value to an organization. They might be the top sales person, highest producer, most creative employee or most reliable go-to person. Perhaps they have a unique and highly coveted skill sought out and valued by consumers and clients – and competitors. "Firing them fast" may result in a significant loss in profits, consumer/client disappointment and a gap in the overall knowledge capital of the organization.

It isn't as simple as "letting them go" because they're causing too much trouble. It is about trying to keep them, if possible, by reinforcing their positive contributions while effectively and defensibly "managing out" their unacceptable and disruptive behaviors.

Second, very few dysfunctional teams are caused by the actions of only one individual. Often, team drama and dysfunction is multi-layered and involves unacceptable behavior and communication on the part of many different team members. Organizations that hastily react to vocal complaints about one leader or employee, by "firing them fast," are shocked and disheartened to see the dysfunction continue, albeit in a different form.

Finally, even where an individual is not seen as adding value to the workplace, leaders are often required to do more than write a letter or sign a check to end the employment relationship. Employees at all levels of organizations are becoming increasingly litigious and vocal after being terminated. In response, leaders are asked to demonstrate – to the courts of justice or courts of public opinion – that they properly, objectively and fairly reviewed the situation before deciding to act.

When leaders rush to judgment and fail to consider the many complexities of workplace dysfunction, they end up paying far more than they would have – in financial, legal, institutional and reputational costs – had they handled the situation fairly in the first instance.

The MIRROR Method allows leaders to keep team members who, while disruptive at one level, add significant contributions at another. The MIRROR Method also empowers leaders to end relationships with those who bring very little value to the organization yet have retained their employment status through control, fear and intimidation.

Regardless of the type of disrespect, disruption or dysfunction involved, the MIRROR Method will show all leaders *how* to act, on a case-by-case and customized basis, to ensure they address unacceptable behavior in a manner that is – and is seen to be – consistently defensible and respectful.

How does *The MIRROR Method* differ from other books on leadership, productivity and workplace conflict? Many leadership books, quite properly, emphasize the importance of healthy and productive workplaces. They stress the many ways in which leaders may not be achieving their goals in relation to team dynamics, efficiencies or profitability. They then, explicitly or by inference, place exclusive responsibility for organizational success on the persuasive abilities of leaders to engage and improve their teams. They convince leaders that if they are articulate enough, compassionate enough, smart enough and put in enough effort, they can win over any and all individuals engaged in disruptive or disrespectful conduct. The unspoken message is that if they fail to do so, the fault lies with the leader.

This analysis, in my view, is unfair, unrealistic and overly simplistic. Ultimately, it would take a magician, not a leader, to control the behavior of others and guarantee they will work well with their teams. Sometimes, even the most effective leaders with the highest of qualifications, experience and skill will be faced with certain individuals who, intentionally or otherwise, perform poorly, behave disruptively, communicate disrespectfully or in some other way fail to "show up" for their team. Leaders should not be blamed for this. Instead, they should be provided with the tools and support in order to address it.

The MIRROR Method is that toolbox and its six steps are the tools.

In brief, the six steps of the MIRROR Method are:

M – MONITOR the workplace for potential signs and symptoms of dysfunction;

I – INQUIRE into the nature and extent of the potential dysfunction, using the MIRROR Triage Process, in order to determine the type of workplace review to conduct;

R – REVIEW the alleged dysfunction objectively, using an informal or formal process (based on the results of the Triage Process);

R – REMEDY the individual dysfunction in accordance with the results of the objective review, using a combination of accountability and support;

O – OPERATIONALLY restore trust, communication and credibility among the team as a whole; and

R – REVISIT the "scene" of the dysfunction to determine whether the remedial and restorative processes were successful.

PART ONE

The Hard Facts Behind the Hardened Workplace

All too commonly, leaders see workplace dysfunction as a relatively minor hiccup in their overall plans for productivity and success. In the face of dysfunction among the team, or with particular individuals, they look for the quick fix, such as hiring a consultant, hosting a team-building day or putting on some training. Do whatever is needed to quickly smooth things over so the organization can move on to more important matters, ones that relate to the financial bottom line. They see workplace dysfunction as wholly unrelated to workplace profitability – and, thus, a much lower priority.

This approach to workplace dysfunction ignores the harsh reality of what many companies now know about workplace dysfunction – not through reading about it, but by surviving through it. Workplace dysfunction, of any type and at any level of the organization, costs companies significant amounts of financial and emotional hardship, which will be outlined below.

The corollary also is true. Workplaces genuinely committed to respectful conduct and communication, transparency and clear accountability of staff and leaders alike face far fewer costs and experience significantly higher levels of productivity and profits. Less drama and less dysfunction result in more deliverables and dollars.

In this Part, we outline the overarching principles that apply throughout the book.

- What is workplace dysfunction?

- Why should leaders care about dysfunction and be genuinely committed to ending it?

- And finally, how can leaders play a critical role in building functional and productive workplaces?

It is fundamental for readers – particularly leaders at all levels of the organization – to understand the bigger picture (as outlined in this Part of the book) before moving on to learn more about the specific dynamics that underlie day-to-day disruption associated with workplace dysfunction.

While every employee is critical to the building of a respectful and thriving workplace, the role and behavior of leadership is critical to the success of any team environment. CEOs, CAOs and executive leaders set the tone for the overall organization. Leaders who report to the executive must ensure they are seen to fully embrace this tone. Frontline employees scrutinize the actions of leaders – at all levels of the organization – with watchful eyes, particularly when it comes to acceptable workplace conduct and communication. If leaders are seen not to value, appreciate or embrace respect, civility and consideration or, worse, are seen to repeatedly engage in disrespectful conduct themselves, then no training course, institutional program or intranet campaign is going to be successful in building a respectful environment.

As will be elaborated on below, leaders must first *talk the talk* when it comes to workplace respect. That is, they must clearly establish what they will and will not tolerate when it comes to acceptable workplace behavior, performance and communication. They then must *walk that talk* – both in ensuring their communication and conduct is consistent with this message and in actively addressing disrespectful and disruptive conduct of others within their organization.

Chapter 1

THE MANY COSTS OF WORKPLACE DYSFUNCTION

The latest headlines – in media or social media – often focus on drama and dysfunction in high-profile workplaces – universities, large corporations and the media outlets themselves.

The details often differ but the underlying story is the same – an employee claims that he or she has suffered from long-standing workplace bullying, sexual harassment or otherwise – and the workplace has done nothing about it.

Dissatisfaction with an organization's response to complaints about dysfunction comes from those who report the concerns as well as those who face the accusations.

Employees who complain about dysfunction often claim they were too afraid to come forward due to perceived fear of retaliation (by the individual, leader or the organization at large); other times, they say they did come forward yet no one listened to them, believed them or helped solve their problem. All too often, they recount that reporting the problem only made the situation worse.

At the same time, many employees accused of dysfunctional conduct often report being treated disrespectfully in response to complaints about their conduct. Many share stories of being silenced and shamed in the face of unfounded accusations, often publicly (through workplace gossip and social media), well before a fair, objective and confidential process has taken place and well before they have been found "guilty" of anything. At a more formal level, many describe being subjected to unfair, reactive and biased investigations conducted by individuals who were either untrained or wrongly motivated in the course of conducting their review.

Workplace dysfunction, complaints of dysfunction and mismanaged responses to such complaints attract significant costs to those individuals and organizations involved, regardless of whose side one is on or which role they might play.

What Is "Workplace Dysfunction" All About?

Many experts who write on the topic of acceptable workplace conduct as well as those organizations who address it often rely on narrow, legalistic definitions regarding human behavior and workplace misconduct, such as human rights violations, personal harassment and workplace bullying.

MYTH: It's better to simply avoid someone than engage in heated discussions.

REALITY: Allowing time to cool off before speaking to someone is acceptable; however, permanently avoiding them – and the issue related to them – is not. Ignoring, excluding or isolating someone is inconsistent with the basic expectations of workplace respect and civility. Difficult or heated discussions are not dysfunctional and do not need to be avoided provided that they are conducted in a respectful manner.

As a result, individuals who genuinely and practically struggle with certain workplace dynamics (related to their leaders, colleagues, customers or otherwise) try to fit their issues into the narrow definitions that have been adopted by the organization as "unacceptable workplace behavior." Those unable to do so are often turned away without being offered support because their "dysfunction" does not align with the organization's specific definitions of unacceptable conduct.

This is not how the MIRROR Method – or any principle within this book – operates. The MIRROR Method is not dependent or contingent on individuals or leaders having to first prove that their concerns or struggles fit within specific, narrow or legalistic definitions of unacceptable conduct.

Rather, this book – and the MIRROR Method – may be applied to *any* behavior, communication, work approach or practice that may be unreasonably interfering with the ability of a team – or specific individuals on the team – to *function* in an effective and productive manner.

Simply put, if any person, practice, process or dynamic is unreasonably interfering with the ability of an individual or team to work, deliver services, produce or function in the interests of the overall organization, then that, by definition, is *workplace dysfunction*.

The types of workplace dysfunction "out there" are broad and varied and commonly depend on the specific personalities of particular individuals and the unique dynamics within teams and workplaces. While bullying/harassment is certainly included on the list, it is but one of many types of dysfunctional behavior. Others include, but are in no way limited to, shunning, hostile/rude communication (through written, verbal and non-verbal communication), persistent gossip, discriminatory or preferential treatment, poor/

negligent performance, erratic attendance/punctuality, safety concerns/breaches, inconsistency or non-compliance with specific policies, processes or procedures and workplace misconduct of a varied nature. Examples of workplace dysfunction are numerous and will be elaborated on further in the chapters that follow.

Figure 1

A CONTEXTUAL APPROACH TO WORKPLACE DYSFUNCTION (EMPLOYEE CONDUCT)

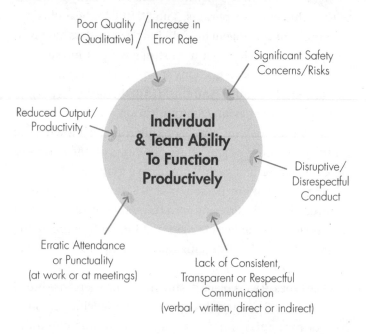

Figures 1 and 2 summarize the various types of "dysfunction" through the many environmental scans that I have conducted over the years. The diagram in Figure 1 reflects the most common dysfunction associated with team members; and Figure 2 reflects dysfunction most commonly associated with leaders.

Figure 2

A CONTEXTUAL APPROACH TO WORKPLACE DYSFUNCTION (LEADER CONDUCT)

In order to place these diagrams in context, consider this example: A team member might be engaged in perceived incompetence or unsafe practices by other team members. This situation then results in concern, resentment and hostility among others, who become impatient with this employee or avoid him/her altogether. The leader may be aware of the situation and simply chooses to ignore it because one or more of the individuals involved is litigious, aggressive or perhaps friends with the leader of the team.

In reviewing Figures 1 and 2, the dysfunction, in this particular example, could potentially include poor performance and safety violations on the part of one team member, unacceptable conduct/communication of other team members and willful or negligent inaction on the part of the leader who has failed to address these dynamics.

At a systemic level, it also could involve poor communication, training or understanding regarding safety or operational processes or inconsistent application of or adherence to such standards throughout the team or organization.

Thus, the overall dysfunction could include a mix of people, processes and practices.

Instead of *The MIRROR Method* defining for readers what is and is not dysfunctional and demanding that behavior fit into narrowly defined, rigid definitions of unacceptable conduct, readers can define for themselves what might be dysfunctional in their workplaces based on the concepts and examples set out in the book. There is no "test" to pass or pre-requisites to meet. If your workplace is practically and genuinely struggling with any unhealthy, disruptive dynamics, then this book – and the MIRROR Method – is for you.

The Dollars Associated with Dysfunction

It would be a mistake to think that "costs" of dysfunction are limited to those that relate to litigation associated with formal claims/grievances.

Well before day-to-day dysfunction turns into a legal issue, it has cost the workplace a fortune in operational and institutional costs.

Beyond the dollars, emotional and personal costs are commonly experienced by every member of the team: the person who is seen as the victim of the dysfunction; the one accused of the dysfunction; the bystanders who, at varying levels, are drawn into or participate in the dysfunction; and the workplace leaders who are expected to vigilantly monitor and fix it.

The costs include the following:

- presenteeism,
- absenteeism,
- low morale and engagement,
- turnover,
- training, overtime and replacement costs, and
- loss of reputation.

PRESENTEEISM

Picture this.

Three members of your team are caught in power struggles and personality differences. Perhaps one of them supervises the other two, although this might not always be so. You see them coming into work so you assume they are working. You see them in an office – or boardroom – and assume they are talking about work or working on work.

Often, none of this is true.

With dysfunction comes office talk – and lots of it. Sometimes, it is mere gossip and speculation about what is going on. Sometimes, it is to vent or provide each other with emotional support. Sometimes, it is to "strategize" on how to prepare for, mitigate or respond to the dysfunctional person's next outburst or disruption.

Regardless, none of it is about work or performing work. And very little of it leads to a constructive, practical and timely resolution of the issues being complained about.

This scenario happens at all levels of organizations, in workplaces everywhere. Well before crystallized complaints of dysfunction hit the leader's desk, turn up in filed grievances/claims or, at worst, become front page news, they have cost the workplace a fortune in lost productivity, reduced engagement and low morale.

Presenteeism is the phenomenon that takes place when staff are at work, but only physically. Mentally, they are not focused on their work. Operationally, they are not performing work. They spend significant amounts of time coping with, addressing and talking about the drama and dysfunction at work rather than, well, working. This results in reduced productivity and decreased focus at work, which affects the department's bottom line in many different ways.

Those directly involved in workplace dysfunction spend time thinking about and coping with the conflict, rather than performing their assigned duties. Their days are spent overthinking the interpersonal dynamics at work in order to come to terms with past disagreements and work to avoid future ones. Worse, they are sometimes planning their vengeance or vindication. As part of this maneuvering, they spend time seeking assistance and support from their colleagues, union or legal representatives, and otherwise.

As they draw in bystanders, supporters and others, the circle of presenteeism expands. Camps are created around and between the perceived victim and alleged perpetrator. The group focuses on the dysfunction/drama at work while work itself is no longer a priority.

Regrettably, presenteeism involves more than misdirected time at work coping with and talking about the dysfunction. In many cases, those involved in the dysfunction become distracted by the destructive dynamics and stop focusing on their work. This often results in costly damage and irreversible errors.

Consider this situation. Three assistants were embroiled in a power struggle over work assignments. They did not listen when their boss, a physician, asked them to call a patient in to discuss her test results. Distracted and upset, the assistants improperly filed away the patient's chart and failed to make the call. The patient wasn't called in for months – and by that time, she was seriously ill. The interpersonal team dysfunction, and resulting lack of focus, only came to light when the clinic was sued for negligence.

In another situation, general laborers encountered a significant "near miss" at a worksite when one of the employees, distracted by a heated argument with a coworker, failed to set up proper safety precautions. Safety regulators performed a random audit at the site and the company was issued significant fines. Luckily, no one was injured.

Stories like this exist in every workplace coping with unmanaged dysfunction. Costs of presenteeism flow not only from individuals not working at all – they also flow from individuals performing their work in an unsafe, sloppy and negligent manner.

ABSENTEEISM

In addition to the costs of presenteeism – that is, employees showing up for work yet not showing up to work – leaders face inordinate costs of employees not showing up for work at all.

The financial costs of workplace absenteeism and sick leave are overwhelming and on the rise. In addition to the cost of sick leave itself, related costs include overtime for relief workers and recruitment costs associated with the hiring and training of new staff.

Many organizations remain unaware of the link between such absenteeism and workplace dysfunction. This link is multi-layered. Workplace dysfunction often causes absenteeism while unmanaged absenteeism often causes workplace dysfunction.

Many workers who experience workplace dysfunction commonly report that they call in sick because of physical or psychological ailments triggered by unresolved issues at their workplace. At the same time, those accused of dysfunctional behavior also call in sick, often in response to the way in which they have been treated or investigated in response to these allegations.

In some of the more extreme cases, bystanders grow extremely fatigued by – and fed up with – the stress and anxiety of being drawn into the drama and dysfunction caused by others. They, too, begin to call in sick in an effort to avoid their very toxic workplace.

If the dysfunction is not remedied, the sick leave worsens, either on an individual or team basis, and employees end up on long-term disability. Dysfunctional departments are commonly associated with high levels of absenteeism, resulting in teams having to run "thin" or "short" because of the number of employees who are unable to work. This scenario, then, contributes to the presenteeism and negligence outlined above and overall productivity significantly declines.

Even when "dysfunction" is not the underlying trigger, excessive and uncontrolled absenteeism is a form of dysfunction itself – which often triggers further dysfunction. Individuals who fail to show up on a regular and consistent basis, by repeatedly calling in sick at the last minute, arriving late or leaving early, end up creating disruption to and disproportionate workloads for those around them. If this situation is not addressed by leaders, resentment and hostility grows among those who have "shown up." This results in further dysfunction, separate and apart from the absenteeism itself.

LOW MORALE AND ENGAGEMENT

In many organizations, individuals are surveyed to assess the level of departmental morale and employee engagement.

When morale and employee engagement drop, workplace leaders are asked to assess what might be going on and are then expected to fix it.

A closer look at the metrics often demonstrates that there is workplace dysfunction and disrespect taking place that is not being adequately detected, acknowledged or remedied by the leaders. It might not be something as extreme as workplace harassment or bullying; it might be a workplace "change" that has not been effectively managed or accepted, a perceived lack of transparency, poor communication or inconsistent practices by leadership or perceptions of favoritism by management. Regardless, dysfunction that does not get addressed does not disappear – it inevitably shows up through disengaged and disheartened staff. Beyond and more important than poor survey outcomes, staff faced with persistent dysfunction attend work on "auto-pilot" and do the bare minimum, no longer giving their all to the work and workplace they once genuinely valued.

TURNOVER

If low engagement/morale scores are measured and then ignored – or not measured at all – the "stars" on the team will leave the department or the organization at large. Many employees report that they turn down attractive opportunities elsewhere when they work in a functional and thriving workplace, with a leader who mentors and supports them; and actively seek out new job opportunities when there is dysfunction that is not being addressed.

Again, it would be a mistake to think that the only employees who leave are those directly involved in the dysfunction. Many employees who are drawn into or held captive by the tension, anxiety and negativity associated with workplace dysfunction also choose to look for opportunities elsewhere.

A positive and respectful workplace environment is valued by many employees and remains a key marker of employee retention; when respect disappears, the competent and highly valued individuals begin looking for options elsewhere.

TRAINING, OVERTIME AND REPLACEMENT COSTS

When individuals go off on sick leave or choose to resign, the workplace faces significant costs associated with hiring relief staff, recruiting, training new staff and paying existing staff overtime in the interim.

LOSS OF REPUTATION

When employees work in a toxic or dysfunctional department or become victims of aggressive or unacceptable behavior by others, they talk about it – a lot. The talk extends beyond the walls of the department in which they work to other internal departments and, often, well outside the organization to other workplaces, through socializing and social media. In extreme cases, the dysfunction hits the news and the story goes viral.

As a result, certain workplaces get tagged as "problem places" to work. Internal employees are reluctant to apply or transfer into those departments and casual employees often refuse to accept shifts there. In many instances, relief employees – nurses, construction workers, emergency dispatchers and others – report that they first ask "who is working" on the shift for which they are being called. If a particular employee or supervisor is working, they refuse the shift. In their words, "the drama and dysfunction isn't worth the money."

At a more global level, individuals are attracted to workplaces that are known for and often formally recognized as being one of the "Top Best Employers."

At the end of the day, despite an organization's invest-ment in job fairs and recruitment campaigns, workplaces will continue to suffer from systemic challenges in attracting and retaining the sharpest and brightest workers if they face a reputation of cultivating and tolerating intolerable behavior.

Chapter 2

WORKPLACE DYSFUNCTION AND THE CHANGING LEGAL LANDSCAPE

The Link Between Leadership Inaction and Workplace Litigation

Team members who have issues with others on their team are often left to their own devices to "work it out themselves." More often than not, they fail to do so. Sometimes it's because they don't want to, sometimes it is because they are too intimidated to do so, but more often than not, it's because they don't know how to.

Instead of assisting the team with an early resolution to their issues, many frontline supervisors and managers "wish away" this dysfunction and place responsibility for it back on the shoulders of staff. This does not solve the problem – it allows it to fester and expand, causing increasing damage to individuals and the team as a whole.

If poor performance, misconduct, disrespect or interpersonal dysfunction is not resolved in an early, fair and objective manner, the issues will worsen and ultimately end up in a legal forum for resolution. Simply put, dysfunction that is not addressed (either by the parties or their leaders) *will* (not *might*) be litigated. The only question is when, by whom and in what forum.

The Dot Versus the Train Wreck:
The Importance of Early Intervention

Many matters that are formally investigated or adjudicated begin with relatively minor dysfunction that was never addressed – an inappropriate or insensitive comment, a misunderstanding, perceived shunning and otherwise. These are considered, in the MIRROR Method – as "Dots" of dysfunction – that is, clearly defined and specific issues that require a practical and early resolution.

Figure 3 illustrates the evolution of workplace dysfunction. When Dots of dysfunction are ignored, they fester over time and eventually become "train wrecks" that affect the entire team. These are called "train wrecks" because, by the time they happen, the carnage is extensive and unmanageable. There is no trust or communication between individuals or on the team generally. Personal, professional and institutional costs abound.

Dots of dysfunction are present in every workplace. Train wrecks only arise when Dots are left unresolved and, instead, are permitted to accumulate.

The issues that show up in a train wreck are often no more complex – factually or legally – than the initial Dots of dysfunction. When Dots are not detected, reviewed or resolved early by frontline staff and leaders, dysfunction associated with the Dot grows and expands. Additional incidents occur and other individuals are drawn in.

In one situation, Employees A and B had a 10-minute heated exchange (about "who" was supposed to do "what"). This left Employee A feeling hurt and angry. He approached

Employee B to discuss the issue. Employee B dismissed Employee A's concerns and told him everything was fine and refused to talk about it further. However, it was clear from Employee B's behavior that it was not "fine." Employee B avoided Employee A and refused to work with or speak to Employee A.

Figure 3
DEALING WITH IT AT THE DOT

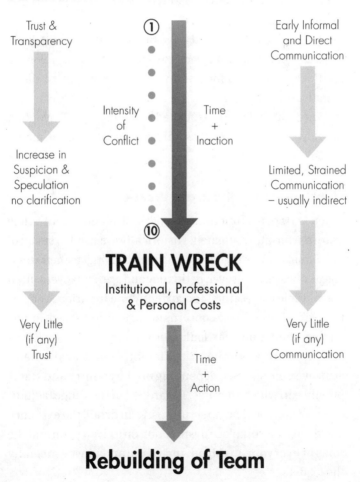

TRAIN WRECK
Institutional, Professional
& Personal Costs

Rebuilding of Team

Employee A sought assistance from his supervisor who promised to "deal with it." However, the supervisor ignored the situation and assumed (hoped) it would go away. The issue did not go away but Employee A did. Eventually, he went off on approved medical leave because of the workplace environment. He also filed a workplace harassment complaint, not because he wanted to, but only because no one was addressing his concerns. His complaint was successful against Employee B and the supervisor who failed to intervene.

This issue likely could have been resolved in a 1-hour facilitated discussion. Instead, it was resolved after a prolonged medical leave and a formal investigation by a third-party adjudicator.

The financial costs associated with Employee B avoiding Employee A and the leader's failure to assist were estimated at $50,000.

The Venues for the Train Wreck

When Dots of dysfunction are not resolved informally, they are often formally litigated. Historically, we used to speak of individuals "choosing" a forum in which to litigate their workplace concerns. However, in this day and age, employees often file multiple complaints, concurrently and in various venues, to have their workplace concerns heard and addressed. Rarely do they choose one particular forum.

There are a number of different venues available to aggrieved employees, depending on the country and state/province in which they live. Regardless of the venue, adjudicators of all types end up scrutinizing, in detail, the existence and degree of workplace dysfunction on a given team and the roles of everyone involved, including and most especially the leaders.

Litigation may be available through one of the venues listed below.

- Union Grievances – Labor Arbitrations
- Workplace Health and Safety Tribunals
- Human Rights/Workplace Discrimination Tribunals
- Employment Standards/Labor Relations Boards
- Privacy Commissions
- Regulatory Bodies
- Courts

UNION GRIEVANCES – LABOR ARBITRATIONS

At one end of the spectrum, individuals commonly file grievances against employers, through their Union, for failing to maintain a harassment-free or discrimination-free workplace. The grievance centers not only on the alleged behaviors of the specific individual involved but also on the employer's role in prolonging the harassment by failing to remedy it in an expedited and appropriate manner.

At the other end of the spectrum, those found "guilty" of unacceptable behavior commonly file grievances in response to discipline they have received following an investigation into their misconduct. These grievances focus on issues surrounding the investigation, including alleged lack of objectivity, neutrality, thoroughness and timeliness. They also focus on the outcome of the investigation by alleging that the discipline was without merit or excessive in nature.

WORKPLACE HEALTH AND SAFETY TRIBUNALS

Employees commonly file complaints with third-party health and safety tribunals alleging that the actions of the employer, or the actions of staff combined with the inaction of the employer, have resulted in a physically or psychologically unsafe workplace.

A number of tribunals allow workers to file claims for compensation related to "injuries" arising from specific or cumulative incidents of workplace dysfunction.

In addition to individual claims, workers often report a "culture" or systemic pattern of unsafe workplace practices. This often triggers a more comprehensive review by the tribunal.

Workplace safety tribunals can have significant legislated powers of entry, inspection and document review and formal authority to issue fines, penalties and mandatory remedial orders.

HUMAN RIGHTS/WORKPLACE DISCRIMINATION TRIBUNALS

Individuals who perceive that they have been discriminated against or harassed at the workplace on the basis of "protected" grounds in human rights/anti-discrimination legislation may file a complaint, against coworkers, leaders and the organization, seeking compensation and related remedial orders. The protected grounds can include gender, age, race, religion, physical and mental disability, political beliefs and, in some jurisdictions, also include sexual orientation, family status and marital status.

Individuals who have been accused of such behaviors also can file complaints of this nature if they can establish that their behavior relates to a protected ground under human rights legislation. For example, if Steve is accused, investigated and subsequently disciplined for engaging in workplace threats, and asserts that his threatening conduct relates to an underlying mental disability, then he may file a complaint arguing that the discipline is discriminatory because it relates to his mental disability. This is not to say his claim will be successful – it is simply to say that, in many jurisdictions, he may be entitled to file a claim – as many employees have done.

EMPLOYMENT STANDARDS/LABOR RELATIONS BOARDS

Depending on the jurisdiction in question, employees may have the option to file complaints with an employment standards or labor relations tribunal if they are of the view that the employer's action contravenes legislated workplace standards.

In some jurisdictions, workers also are permitted to file complaints against their unions if they believe the union has failed to sufficiently represent their interests at the workplace or has somehow treated them in an arbitrary or discriminatory manner. This can happen if workplace dysfunction arises between two union members and one of them perceives the union to be "favoring" the other in its overall handling of the matter.

PRIVACY COMMISSIONERS

In many jurisdictions, employees may file complaints with privacy commissioners if they believe their personal privacy has been breached in the workplace or if they think that there is relevant personal information about them that the employer has failed to disclose to them.

Complaints of this nature commonly arise in the course of and following formal investigations and reviews regarding workplace dysfunction.

REGULATORY BODIES

Individuals who are members of professional societies may face complaints to their regulatory body/committee, arguing that their conduct not only constitutes workplace harassment or misconduct, it also contravenes their professional code of ethics. Such regulatory bodies are associated with many professional groups, such as law societies, colleges of physicians, teachers and nurses, associations of professional engineers and institutes of chartered accountants.

COURTS

In some jurisdictions, employees in non-unionized workplaces (and excluded leaders within unionized workplaces) may file claims of "constructive dismissal" alleging that their workplace environment is so disrespectful and unsupportive that they have been forced to quit. They then seek severance as if they had, in fact, been dismissed without cause. They also may seek damages for intentional infliction of mental distress, interference in contractual relations and otherwise.

Alternatively, non-unionized employees who believe they were disciplined or terminated without merit (or as a result of an unfair investigation into allegations against them) can file a civil claim for damages on the basis of constructive/ wrongful dismissal. Included in this complaint or as a separate action altogether, they may allege damages for defamation for loss of reputation flowing from the allegations, investigation, outcome or a combination of all three.

With each complaint, regardless of which venue, comes significant costs, including fees of legal counsel and other experts involved, as well as lost production time associated with pre-litigation preparation and attendance at the proceeding itself.

Expanding the Legal Inquiry: A Systematic Approach to Adjudicating Workplace Dysfunction

While the specific legal requirements associated with a respectful, harassment-free workplace will vary from jurisdiction to jurisdiction, there is a growing and significant intolerance – socially and legally – for systemic mistreatment of employees, workplace toxicity, discrimination and bullying, most especially when basic human rights and dignity are being violated.

Historically (and regrettably in some current workplaces and regimes), there were few restrictions on workplace behavior, particularly when it came to those with institutional and political power. The focus was (or is) on "pay for work" with little consideration for the overall environment in which that work took (or takes) place.

Over time, with significant contributions from labor movements and advocacy groups associated with women's rights, human rights and worker safety, there has been increased legal scrutiny of and enhanced expectations related to the respectful treatment of workers.

Regardless of which venue, forum or jurisdiction is involved, the actions of the individuals and teams involved in the alleged workplace dysfunction will be closely reviewed and evaluated. Adjudicators will commonly ask these questions.

- What is the history and context associated with the complaint being filed?

- Who, at the workplace, knew about this incident, in whole or in part? What role did they play (i.e., were they leaders, instigators, victims, bystanders?)

- When did they first know of the potential dysfunction?

- Did they contribute to the dysfunction through their inaction/action and in what way?

- Did they attempt to resolve or report the dysfunction? What was the outcome of this?

- If they didn't take any action, why not?

- If it took a long time to act, why the delay?

- Who was responsible for what part of the dysfunction and to what degree? This may include individuals outside the team, in other departments and may involve contractors, clients and members of the public.

The analysis flowing from these queries often focuses on the roles and responsibilities of *everyone* involved in the alleged dysfunction. No one's conduct is immune from review.

- **Complainant**: An objective review will look at the role of the complainant, specifically, whether he/she came forward in a timely and confidential manner and whether actions were taken by the complainant that either mitigated or aggravated the damage initially caused by the respondent's alleged misconduct.

- **Respondent/Accused**: An objective review will look at the role of the respondent and whether the respondent engaged in behavior that objectively and legally constitutes "misconduct" (as alleged or otherwise) and whether there is a "defense" that in some way mitigates the respondent's actions.

- **Bystanders:** An objective review will look at the role of bystanders to determine what they observed and what they did in response.

Most significantly, the review looks closely at the role of workplace leaders to determine what they did in the face of observed or reported dysfunction. Adjudicators commonly determine when the leader knew – or should have known

– about the dysfunction in question and what that leader did in an effort to remedy the situation.

MYTH: Respect is the sole responsibility of leadership.

REALITY: Respect is the responsibility of everyone in the workplace, including complainants, respondents, bystanders and third parties (clients, customers, contractors, members of the public).

The Legal Expectations of Leaders

Leaders are increasingly expected to play a critical and active role in setting the overall tone of the workplace and in creating a respectful and productive environment.

They are expected to do so in three key respects.

1. Create and support a respectful and productive workplace
2. Act as a role model
3. Hold others accountable

CREATE AND SUPPORT A RESPECTFUL AND PRODUCTIVE WORKPLACE

First, leaders must clearly and firmly establish, communicate and fully support the expectations of the organization surrounding respectful conduct, communication and treatment of and by all individuals within the organization.

Leaders must make it clear that these expectations constitute *non-negotiable standards and expectations* for everyone who works for or interacts with those employed by the organization. Respect and civility are the foundation of any successful workplace and it is up to the leaders to communicate this message to others.

The seriousness with which this message is viewed is dependent on the seriousness with which it is conveyed. Its success is wholly contingent on genuine and clear communication from the executive team/senior leadership. The message should not be contracted out to a communications consultant or PR firm. Nor should it be delegated to human resources. This messaging sets the standard for how everyone in the organization is expected to operate. In order for it to be seen as credible and persuasive, communication about respect must come from senior leadership and be presented in a substantive and meaningful way.

The overall message regarding the importance of workplace respect and the specific expectations regarding acceptable conduct must then be fully adopted and communicated by middle managers and frontline leaders. Anyone who is a leader, or seen to be in a position of leadership, of any type and at any level, must echo and support the expectations established by the senior executives.

ACT AS A ROLE MODEL

Second, all leaders must "walk the talk" of workplace respect and civility. In the eyes of the law – and frontline employees being managed – leaders are seen as role models and are expected to act accordingly. No message about the importance of or need for civility and respect will be seen or accepted as credible if leaders act in a manner inconsistent with this message.

All too often, certain leaders mistakenly assume that if they hold a position of authority or power, the rules, particularly those surrounding respect and civility, do not apply to them. This is not the case. In fact, it is quite the opposite. Leaders are expected to act with a greater degree of civility and respect than others within the organization.

A leader who does not "role model" appropriate conduct and communication may well expose the organization to significant criticism and liability in three respects.

First, leaders are held to a higher standard of care by third-party adjudicators. If leaders are accused of inappropriate conduct, they often face increased scrutiny (as does the overall organization), given their elevated position, power and authority within the establishment.

Second, when leaders do not model appropriate behavior or adhere to workplace expectations surrounding respect and civility, it is often challenging (and uncommon) for staff to take seriously any message regarding the "need" for workplace respect, to the overall detriment of the environment. Others model the behavior of their leaders – good or bad – rude or polite – regardless of the formal "party line" concerning appropriate workplace conduct.

Third, when an organization holds individual staff members accountable for disrespect or incivility, an increasingly common – and commonly successful – defense is not that the behavior did not happen or that it was somehow acceptable but, rather, that particular leaders in the organization engage in the same or similar behavior. If this is confirmed, the staff member's discipline often is considered "discriminatory" and overturned on this basis.

HOLD OTHERS ACCOUNTABLE

The third way in which leaders play a critical role in the context of respect and civility is to hold staff accountable for inappropriate behavior. A core responsibility of leadership is to ensure that staff comply with the standards and expectations of the organization regarding performance, behavior, communication or otherwise.

Once leaders establish and communicate expectations

to staff, they are expected to ensure that those expectations are met – consistently and regularly – by *all* members of their team. Those who fail to meet expectations should be addressed in a measured, respectful and escalating manner to ensure the environment remains functional for the overall team.

Staff who experience dysfunctional conduct from their colleagues commonly complain about leaders who are aware of this dysfunction but do nothing to stop it (or become involved far too late). This concern is shared by many third-party adjudicators who are subsequently tasked to review these complaints.

In order for individuals to respect the organization's messaging surrounding respect and take seriously expectations regarding performance, communication and behavior, they must see leaders respond in a timely and effective manner to actions that are inconsistent with these expectations.

MYTH: Leaders can ignore anonymous complaints.

REALITY: Leaders are expected to inquire into potential dysfunction in the workplace. If an anonymous complaint gives the leader sufficient information to make inquiries, then those inquiries must be made. The fact that the complaint is anonymous does not, on its own, justify inaction on the part of the leader.

Leaders who are "blind" to dysfunction on their team create:

- damage to their credibility and respect as leaders;
- damage to the team caused by the continuing dysfunction of the individual who is not being held accountable by leadership; and

- an overall crisis of credibility in relation to the organization's commitment to workplace respect and civility, given the apparent unwillingness of the leadership team to take on and address those who act in a manner contrary to this commitment.

The MIRROR Method is an accessible, practical and effective method to use to properly diagnose and remedy any and all unacceptable and dysfunctional dynamics on a team and any unacceptable conduct or performance on the part of team members. However, it cannot "run" itself. The MIRROR Method's success in building and maintaining a productive and respectful workplace lies in the hands of its leaders – leaders who clearly establish and communicate fundamental expectations of productivity, respect and civility, leaders who model these expectations through their own conduct and communication and leaders who consistently, clearly and fairly hold team members accountable for acting in a manner inconsistent with these expectations.

The Bottom Line on the Bottom Line

Dysfunction is costing organizations a fortune. Sometimes, it triggers the breakdown of an entire team. Sometimes, it causes irreparable damage to professional and personal lives and ends working relationships.

It is not only practically and financially sound to end workplace dysfunction, it has now become a legal reality.

From the barracks to the bank to the boardroom, leaders can no longer turn a blind eye to the drama and dysfunction that defines and disrupts them and their teams. It is time to act.

Chapter 3

UNDERSTANDING THE SCOPE OF DYSFUNCTION: IS IT A "BAD DAY" OR A "BAD LIFE"

Many conflict management programs offer leaders a "quick fix" to their workplace drama and dysfunction. Common marketing slogans include catch phrases like "three simple ways to resolve conflict on your team" or "a weekend workshop to put an end to workplace drama." The list goes on. This often is misleading, could expose your organization to unnecessary costs and ultimately results in less than stellar outcomes.

Why?

1. **No Quick Fixes:** First, there is no quick fix to conflict management. In my 20+ years of working with struggling teams, frustrated leaders and dissatisfied employees, I have yet to discover a one-size-fits-all approach that will work in every situation, with any leader or employee and in every industry. Both the law – and the practical realities of modern-day workplaces – demand that leaders adopt an individualized and customized

approach to remedying workplace dysfunction that considers the unique history, context and culture of each particular situation.

2. **First-Aid is Not Enough:** Second, many approaches to conflict management invest in and focus upon quick fixes to "solve" the "problem" between team members. Although this first-aid approach has some initial attraction, ultimately it is a waste of money and time. It is not of any benefit to address an issue that has not been fairly and objectively assessed or properly diagnosed; intervening in the absence of an objective review often makes the situation worse. Organizations – and their leaders – need to understand the dynamics at play and the potential layers of dysfunction before trying to fix them. A clear assessment and diagnosis of the issues involved will significantly increase the likelihood of reaching a successful and sustainable resolve.

3. **Gradients of Dysfunction:** Finally, there are many different types of workplace dysfunction, which vary in severity and frequency. Not all dysfunction should be responded to with the same level of urgency or formality or remedied in the same way.

While it is critical that leaders "act" in the face of dysfunction, the first step in that "action," perhaps ironically, is to refrain from acting. They need to "push the pause button" and understand what is going on before trying to fix it.

The first step to take in understanding workplace dysfunction is to determine where a particular incident or situation might fall on the the Scale of Dysfunctional Conduct (see Figure 4).

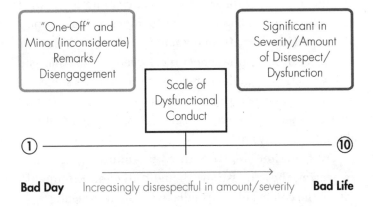

Figure 4

SCALE OF DYSFUNCTIONAL CONDUCT

"One-Off" and Minor (inconsiderate) Remarks/ Disengagement

Scale of Dysfunctional Conduct

Significant in Severity/Amount of Disrespect/ Dysfunction

① ———————————————————— ⑩

Bad Day   Increasingly disrespectful in amount/severity   **Bad Life**

Understanding the Scale of Dysfunctional Conduct

As we have discussed in earlier chapters, dysfunctional conduct is a broad term and includes any interaction, behavior, communication, attitude, practice or procedure that interferes with the healthy and productive functioning of an individual on a team or a team as a whole.

As set out in Figure 1, A Contextual Approach to Workplace Dysfunction (Employee Conduct) (in Chapter 1), based on the many scans I have performed and interventions that I have conducted over the years, the most common types of dysfunctional conduct that show up in dysfunction among employees include: disrespectful communication (including all types of written, oral and non-verbal communication to or about others in the workplace), disruptive or disrespectful conduct/behavior, unsafe work practices, lack of communication at all (shunning, isolation, refusal to share information), poor performance, poor productivity, poor attendance, poor punctuality and otherwise.

This is not to suggest – in any way – that other types of dysfunction do not exist. Again, whether or not something or someone is unreasonably and objectively interfering with the ability of an individual or team to function is a question of fact and may vary from team to team and workplace to workplace. It is important not to get locked into specific lists of dysfunctional conduct or we miss the point. Is someone functioning as expected in the workplace? If not, why not? Is the team meeting its mandate and delivering on its deliverables? If not, why not?

Dysfunction is best defined by inquiring into and answering these questions thoughtfully and thoroughly within the context of a particular work environment.

Understanding the "Spectrum" of Dysfunction

Not every annoying or upsetting interaction or remark by an employee or leader will make it on to the Scale of Dysfunctional Conduct. It becomes dysfunctional only when the specific conduct *unreasonably* and *objectively* interferes with the ability of an individual or team to function effectively. This is determined by conducting a proper workplace review (see Step 3, Conducting the Review in Part Three).

One-off comments that are not sufficiently "serious" or disruptive will rarely cause *any* lasting disruption to individuals or the team. However, one-off comments of a vulgar, scathing, threatening, racist or sexual nature might cause disruption sufficient to interfere with the work environment. In those circumstances, it likely will fall on to the Scale. But where?

In determining where the dysfunction might fall on the Scale, it is important to consider two factors, separately and together. First, how potentially serious is the specific inter-action, dynamic or behavior? Second, how often does it occur as between particular individuals or by specific team members or leaders?

Figure 5

THE FOUNDATION OF A RESPECTFUL WORKPLACE

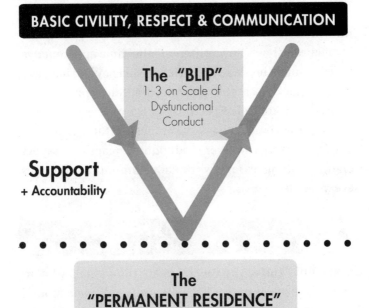

BASIC CIVILITY, RESPECT & COMMUNICATION

The "BLIP"
1- 3 on Scale of Dysfunctional Conduct

Support
+ Accountability

The "PERMANENT RESIDENCE"
8-10 on Scale of Dysfunctional Conduct

Accountability
+ Support

If the behavior or communication is found to be mild in nature and occurs relatively infrequently, it likely will fall on the mild end of the scale. If it is mild yet occurs repeatedly by one person or is targeted towards another repetitively, then it will fall in the middle or severe end of the scale. If it has not occurred previously, but is – standing alone – serious and significant (a death threat for example), then it also will likely fall on the severe end of the scale.

It is important to note that it is not the communication or behavior, *per se*, that will determine where it falls on the Scale. The specific conduct needs to be understood in its proper context considering the intensity and frequency of the conduct, both in general or as directed towards specific individuals.

Figure 5 shows how "different" the same apparent dysfunction might be, depending on its frequency and intensity.

The black box at the top of the diagram represents the critical foundation of respectful workplaces. Every workplace that strives to build and maintain a respectful environment needs to ensure that every individual engages in respect, civility and necessary workplace communication with everyone else.

1-3 ON THE SCALE = THE "BLIPPERS" HAVING A "BAD DAY"

At the mild end of the spectrum are individuals who are having a "bad day or two." They come in and stomp around, act "huffy" or perhaps don't say a word at all, making it difficult for others to work with, rely on or be near them. They may be impatient, non-responsive, sarcastic or irritable. They might be loud and overbearing or completely disengaged.

What is important to note in this scenario is that this conduct or communication is *out of the norm* for the individuals involved. Typically, they meet the expectations of civility and respect in how they treat, interact, work with and serve others. Usually, they cooperate and collaborate with others on their team.

However, on a particular day, or week, they are "not themselves" and their conduct or behavior then interferes with the workplace environment and the overall functioning of the team. Their behavior "drops" are neither respectful nor civil. Their leaders and colleagues are often surprised by this conduct and often note (to themselves and/or each other), "What's with so and so?" By asking this very question, they have made a key observation – that this is a marked difference from how this person usually operates and shows up at work.

After some time, the "blippers" return to their "usual selves" and begin again to engage with others in a respectful and civil manner.

8-10 OUT OF 10 = THE "BAD LIFERS" WHO CONSISTENTLY CREATE DYSFUNCTION

At the other end of the spectrum are those individuals who are having a bad life and often create bad work lives for those working on or leading their team. Day in and day out, they fail to meet the expectations of civility and respect or fail to meet the core expectations of their role within the organization. Perhaps they are persistently rude, dismissive or unpredictable. Perhaps they are consistently disruptive, sloppy or unsafe. Perhaps they are negative and nosey. In contrast to individuals who are having a bad day, these individuals engage in dysfunctional practices *all of the time* either in relation to specific individuals or towards the team as a whole.

In fact, those who work with these individuals have learned to accept their poor performance, conduct or communication and, in fact, have come to expect it. When new individuals join the team – and are understandably perplexed and concerned by these dynamics – others on the team, including the leaders, commonly excuse the inexcusable by saying, "Oh, well, that's just so and so."

By saying this, they have essentially accepted that the dysfunction, as objectively unacceptable and unreasonable as it might be, *is the norm* for this person. Condoning it has become the *norm for the team.*

Disrespectful conduct at this end of the spectrum often meets the definition of workplace bullying/harassment.

3-7 OUT OF 10 = THE RELAPSERS

In the middle of the spectrum are those individuals who are engaged in dysfunctional behavior far more frequently than those having an occasional bad day/week. However, their conduct has not become sufficiently severe or frequent to constitute workplace bullying/harassment. They certainly know how to behave respectfully and with civility, and often do so, but regularly relapse into disrespect and dysfunction.

Individuals in this category are responsible for contributing to a disrespectful/dysfunctional workplace and need to be held accountable for their "blips" into disrespect and drama. Otherwise, over time, their dysfunctional behavior worsens in severity or becomes more frequent.

Staff members who are at the 3-7 level are commonly (and mistakenly) described as "just taking it to the line but not crossing it." Leaders at the 3-7 level are commonly (and mistakenly) described as having a "direct or challenging management style." Both are inaccurate. Individuals – staff or leaders – at 3-7 are not engaged in bullying/harassment but are often significant contributors to a disrespectful or dysfunctional team environment and need to be held

accountable for their disruptive behavior, performance and/
or communication each time it arises.

The Risk of a One-Size-Fits-All Approach

Workplaces that have adopted the one-size-fits-all approach
– and have failed to understand the many nuances and degrees
of workplace dysfunction – have inadvertently made many
situations worse not better.

A team member who comes in and slams the door *once* or
drops the occasional "F-bomb" is often treated in the same
way as a team member who does it *repeatedly*. This is unfair
and, in itself, is a sign of dysfunctional leadership. Individuals who are at 1-3 on the Scale should not be treated in the
same way as those who are at 8-10.

At the same time, an individual who repeatedly rolls his/
her eyes at anyone who ever questions or challenges him/her,
and uses this as a way to silence and intimidate others, may
well be engaging in conduct that falls at 8-10 on the Scale.
However, some workplaces will look solely at the conduct
(that is, the eye-rolling) and indicate this is "not serious" and
inaccurately treat it as a 1-3 issue.

It is critical to assess not the behavior itself, but where the
behavior falls on the Scale, before determining next steps.

CUSTOMIZING THE RESPONSE TO BAD DAYS AND BAD LIVES

The key to addressing those who are "blipping out" and
having a bad day is to provide clear feedback, support and
expectations to them as soon as reasonably possible – in a
respectful, fair and discreet manner.

Often, coworkers and leaders talk themselves out of
acknowledging dysfunction at 1-3 in order to avoid having to

engage in a difficult/challenging discussion with a coworker with whom they usually get along.

However, ignoring the dysfunction and avoiding this discussion does not solve the problem. If someone's behavior or performance has genuinely affected someone else's ability to work, has impacted their overall work environment or has truly interfered with the person's ability to "function," then the dynamic between them shifts. The person affected by the person having a "bad day" has an altered lens about that person, based not only on "what happened" but also on the story they have told themselves about what happened. Their story is often not as accurate as they think. However, they can only discover this by approaching the other person directly to discuss their concerns and perceptions around what transpired.

Instead of addressing the dysfunction, the person who is offended commonly and sometimes unknowingly begins to treat the person having a bad day differently – either through avoidance or by engaging in cautious or dysfunctional behavior themselves. The person having the "bad day" then observes this person (or the overall team) treating them differently. Their lens then becomes affected by this "change" and they too, tell themselves a story about what has happened.

In the absence of clear and direct communication, this distorted cycle of dysfunctional conduct, hurt feelings and inaccurate personal narratives builds and worsens over time. If not addressed, over time, a 1-3 scenario can turn into an 8-10 on the Scale.

Contrary to the assumptions of others on the team, individuals who are at 1-3 and engaged in a "blip" often are not aware of:

- how they are showing up at work (in terms of their behavior, performance or otherwise);

- how their behavior or communication is impacting those around them; or

- how their behavior, performance or communication is interfering with the ability of the team to get work done effectively and productively.

This needs to be shared with them as early as possible and in a clear, direct and respectful manner.

Leaders and staff who observe someone having a "bad day" and choose to talk about them and react negatively towards them are themselves engaging in dysfunctional and disruptive behavior. Gossiping and complaining about, or shunning and avoiding individuals who are at 1-3 on the Scale is as disruptive and dysfunctional as the conduct of that individual. "Secret" dialogue about a person does not help them understand how they are coming across or assist them in stopping their disruptive behavior. It often only serves to make matters worse and spiral out of control.

In the face of bad days/blippers, team members/leaders should use the ideas outlined below.

- Have a MIRROR conversation with the person by talking to him/her directly and confidentially, providing specific, neutral, descriptive, non-inflammatory feedback about what they have said or done, how it is coming across and how it is affecting the other person/team.

- Acknowledge, in a compassionate manner, that this conduct appears to be out of the ordinary for him/her and does not reflect how they usually "show up" for the team.

- Ask if there is any outstanding issue or concern that needs to be resolved from their perspective. "Reality check" the personal stories or narratives that have been attributed to the dysfunctional conduct. Sometimes, the bad day is, in fact, caused by an unresolved conflict that has been allowed to fester between two or more individuals at work. Sometimes, however, it has nothing at all to do with anyone at work. This can only be determined by "checking in" with the person having the bad day.

- Work with each other to determine how to "function" more effectively moving forward.

- If the behavior continues after this discussion, the matter needs to be escalated to the leader.

- Individuals (both initiators and responders) can have others attend with them for the MIRROR conversation, for support.

In addition, leaders who engage in discussions with those having a bad day need to remind them that, regardless of why they are having their bad day/week (which is often legitimate and sometimes very misfortunate), they are expected to respectfully communicate and cooperate with their team and others while at work. Leaders should ask how they can assist the employee work through their bad day in a way that allows them – and others – to get the work done in a productive manner.

Senior leaders need to participate in this MIRROR conversation if it is the frontline leader who is having a bad day/week.

TREATING A BAD LIFE LIKE A BAD DAY

Staff, including leaders, who repeatedly engage in rude, dismissive, disruptive or disrespectful behavior towards others, need to be treated far differently than the person having a one-off, bad day or week. Support and clarity for a person having a bad day – at 1-3 – makes sense. However, support for someone who is having a "bad life" – at 8-10 on the Scale – is akin to indefensible enabling and condonation of unacceptable behavior, performance and communication.

If unacceptable behavior and practices have become an institutional and expected "norm" for certain individuals, then senior leadership, including boards, executives, CEOs and CAOs, must become involved. An objective review must take place and, if concerns are founded, a formal and comprehensive plan of personal and professional accountability needs to be implemented. Success in addressing individuals at this end of the spectrum demands consistent, courageous and clear leadership, which includes a formalized system of expectations and escalating consequences when those expectations are not met.

In contrast to MIRROR conversations at 1-3, accountability at 8-10 is not a task for coworkers nor should it be left to one frontline supervisor or manager to remedy. Individuals at the bad-life end of the spectrum need to be managed by a comprehensive leadership team.

THE RELAPSERS

Individuals whose behavior, performance or communication falls within the mid-point of the spectrum need a combination of support and accountability. As soon as they relapse, they need to be given the same clarity and support as those at the bad-day end of the spectrum. However, in the face of their continual return to unacceptable conduct, their bad-day behaviors need to be addressed through a system of formal reviews and escalating accountability. (This will be further outlined in Step 4 of the MIRROR Method, Designing and Implementing Individual Remedies.)

How Does the Scale of Dysfunctional Conduct Apply to Leadership?

While a number of complaints against leaders focus on a failure to act in response to coworker/team dysfunction, many also focus on dysfunctional, disrespectful and discriminatory conduct of leaders themselves.

MYTH: In the name of transparency and trust, leaders should let individuals know that they are "dealing with" particular staff.

REALITY: Leaders can assure staff that they are taking concerns seriously and should advise staff of informal or formal reviews that require their involvement; however, at no time should leaders disclose confidential personnel information (disciplinary or non-disciplinary) about one staff member to others.

Board members, executive teams and senior leadership need to be well-versed in understanding and applying this scale to each other and to their middle management and supervisory teams to ensure that all leaders are consistently "walking the talk" of respect, professionalism and accountability with their teams.

Leaders are not exempt from the many legal expectations surrounding respectful and professional behavior and communication. As outlined previously, there is a higher standard of care and more rigorous legal expectations applied to the conduct and communication of individuals in positions of authority.

Significantly, while many dysfunctional leadership practices do not meet the extreme definitions of bullying/

harassment, a number of them fall within 3-8 and need to be remedied. These communication practices and behaviors are commonly associated with "weak leadership" or "challenging management styles."

As set out in Figure 2, A Contextual Approach to Workplace Dysfunction (Leader Conduct) (in Chapter 1), the most common types of dysfunctional conduct that show up in team dysfunction caused by leaders include:

- lack of clear communication to staff regarding workplace changes, strategic direction or otherwise;

- a lack of clear decisive direction to staff or, conversely, ever-changing direction to staff;

- different staff members receiving different information;

- different staff members receiving different direction (or a different response from the leader) on the same issues;

- a perception of preferential or differential treatment towards certain staff based on personal as opposed to work-related reasons (friendships, falling outs, likeability, malleability);

- inconsistent interpretation and application of rules and regulations, commonly seen as being connected to the person not the practices;

- being on the "outs" with certain staff, targeting certain staff and blocking them out of opportunities (directly or more subtly);

- lack of genuine consultation with staff on changes to policies and procedures;

- lack of responsiveness to staff queries, questions and concerns;

- lack of clear or timely decision-making due to an institutional/systemic/cultural fear of making mistakes or a general lack of empowerment to make decisions;

- excessive control and micromanagement of staff in relation to day-to-day operations and decisions;

- lack of acknowledgment of staff contribution to team success – not "sharing the stage;"

- a practice of blaming staff for mistakes and an unwillingness to accept responsibility for team weaknesses or errors;

- leaders talking about personal or professional issues involving one staff member to other staff;

- leaders providing critical feedback to staff in front of other staff, customers or clients;

- leaders engaged in personalized attacks or sarcastic "digs" towards staff in the name of "discipline" or "coaching;" and

- leaders pitting staff against each other (inviting staff to monitor each other, encouraging staff to report each other).

It is behavior like this, in contrast to the more extreme type of conduct associated with bullying and harassment that creates widespread dysfunction on the team, and often triggers dysfunctional behavior between and among team members. This ultimately causes shining stars to leave, while creating huge and often irreparable rifts among those left behind.

THE DIFFERENCE BETWEEN "DYSFUNCTION" AND "CONFLICT"

Conflict is very different than dysfunction and is not necessarily dysfunctional. In fact, heated debates, intense "conflicts" and significant challenges to the status quo often act as catalysts to progressive change in an individual or team. Unfortunately, in many organizations, conflict in this context is not properly understood, valued or encouraged.

Some leaders assume that conflict in the form of interpersonal disagreements, differing philosophies or political viewpoints, formal grievances, general challenges to or questioning of leadership decisions or practices is a sign of a dysfunctional team or insubordination by its members. As a result, they assume that, to demonstrate a healthy workplace, conflict and disagreements must be eliminated or silenced. Consensus (or the perception of consensus) is equated with workplace "respect" and becomes the goal, at any cost. Challenges to the status quo are seen as "issues" that require immediate intervention by leadership, often by being silenced as opposed to resolved.

Teams in this type of environment describe a yes-sir/madam mentality where they are expected to unquestioningly follow direction just because the leader said so. Alternatively, they describe a disingenuous all-for-one-and-one-for-all culture where positivity is mandated at whatever cost. At its worst, they describe a culture of fear where individuals face serious repercussions (some more subtle than others) for "rocking the boat" of false consensus. Those who question policy, procedure or practices are seen as "troublemakers" whereas those who "go with the flow" and blindly "agree" with the status quo are commonly put on the path of social acceptance and workplace success.

This approach overlooks a number of important points. The presence of conflict, in and of itself, is not *necessarily* a negative force or the cause of team dysfunction. Disagreements, debates and the ability to question the status quo are not and should not be seen as dynamics that need to be eliminated. In fact, they are necessary and vital components of workplaces that strive to remain cutting edge and progressive. A culture of excellence demands that workplaces facilitate and encourage challenging and difficult conversations, including support for those that question the status quo.

The converse of this is that the absence of "conflict" is not *necessarily* a sign of a functional and healthy team. Many "grievance-free" workplaces are often the result of one or more aggressive and overly controlling leaders or team members who silence anyone who disagrees with them, either because they feel threatened by being challenged or are obsessed with the need to control the workplace. Quite often, staff do not complain because they are too fearful to challenge the leaders or colleagues involved. Instead, the impacted individuals leave or stay underground. Rather than rock the boat, staff (often the top performers) disembark altogether.

Grievance-free dysfunctional workplaces are commonly associated with high rates of turnover, low staff retention and low engagement/morale.

Thus "conflict" is not synonymous with "dysfunction." Conflict becomes dysfunctional only when it is managed, discussed and resolved in a *disrespectful* manner. That is, if, during the course of having a disagreement or attempting to resolve differences, individuals engage in disrespectful, personalized attacks of others – either during the discussions or afterwards, either to their faces or behind their backs – they are behaving in a dysfunctional manner that needs to be addressed.

MYTH: Disagreements between team members mean that the "team" is dysfunctional.

REALITY: Disagreements (differences of opinion, opposing viewpoints, etc.) do not, on their own, constitute evidence of dysfunction. The existence of dysfunction will depend on *how* individuals communicate with and about each other – and how they treat each other – during and following these "disagreements."

While minimizing such *dysfunctional behavior* is critical to the development of a respectful workplace, reaching *consensus* is not. Teams that have guidelines on how individuals will *treat* each other in the course of debates and difficult discussions as well as clear roles and responsibilities in relation to decision-making processes will avoid dysfunction even in the absence of unanimity.

THE DIFFERENCE BETWEEN "DYSFUNCTION" AND "BULLYING"

Similar to the confusion surrounding conflict in the workplace, there also is misuse of the term "bullying" and misunderstanding regarding the differences between "dysfunction," and "bullying."

In many workplaces, there is an assumption that disagreements and critical feedback – between staff or from leaders to staff – constitute a form of workplace bullying. If someone criticizes someone else's work or disputes the validity of their findings/opinions, they will be accused of bullying. This negative branding of critical feedback and open dialogue has led to a fear of challenging others or engaging in direct, transparent discussions with them.

Legally, the mere fact that someone disagrees with someone else or offers critical commentary about work-related issues does not mean that they are a bully *or* engaging in dysfunctional behavior.

MYTH: Performance management is a valid exercise of management's rights and does not constitute harassment/bullying.

REALITY: The actual "performance management" or discipline is not, in itself, evidence of harassment/bullying. However, if the performance management or discipline is carried out or implemented in a disrespectful or demeaning manner, then it likely falls somewhere on the Scale of Dysfunctional Conduct. If the severity of that dysfunction falls at 9 or 10 on the Scale, then it would constitute harassment/bullying.

Second, even if someone, in the course of a disagreement, has acted in a less than perfect and somewhat dysfunctional manner, it does not mean that the person is a *bully*. I share a key mantra here: *a bad day does not a bully make*. As we have discussed, there is a range of dysfunctional behavior that happens in every workplace. Bullying and harassment falls at 8-10 on the Scale of Dysfunctional Conduct. The mere fact that a message could have been delivered or received more appropriately or respectfully does not necessarily confirm the presence of "bullying."

All attitudes, communication, behaviors and performance issues that unreasonably and objectively interfere with the functioning of individuals and/or a team are dysfunctional; but not all such behaviors are bullying. It is important to know the difference and use the term "bullying" with care.

Bullying is a loaded term, with serious personal and professional consequences, and needs to be applied with respectful caution.

It's All About the "How" – The Many Faces and Fonts of Workplace Dysfunction

The root of most complaints surrounding workplace dysfunction is the manner in which individuals have been treated; that is, *how* others have behaved towards them, *how* messages have been communicated or delivered and *how* leadership decisions have been implemented. The "rub" is often not found in the content of the disagreement but, rather, in the surrounding behaviors. How often do we hear, "It's not what they *said* that bothered me, it's *how* they said it."

When it comes to workplace dysfunction, it is all about the *how*. *How* individuals are treated at the workplace – by coworkers, leaders, customers or otherwise – will most commonly determine whether or not a disagreement or discussion is cast as dysfunctional. *How often* they are treated in this dysfunctional way will determine where it falls on the Scale of Dysfunctional Conduct and whether or not it constitutes workplace bullying.

DIRECT AND INDIRECT DYSFUNCTION

Workplace dysfunction may be "direct" – that is, directed at the person involved, either in writing or verbally, in person or on the phone, in front of others or in private. Note that the mere fact there are no witnesses does not make it any less dysfunctional and is not a legitimate or credible basis for inaction on the part of others, especially leaders.

Disrespectful communication, of late, is often "indirect" in nature. Workplaces are filled with staff and leaders who routinely speak and write *about* others, not *to* them. In some situations, the simple act of speaking or writing *about* another individual rather than *to* them is, in itself, a sign of dysfunction and disrespect.

This behavior becomes that much more dysfunctional when the person who is being discussed is described or characterized in a disrespectful manner or in a manner that potentially breaches his/her personal privacy (e.g. it involves a personnel issue, a personal matter, a medical condition or otherwise).

Dysfunction also can be indirect when individuals gossip to spread drama, divisiveness and dysfunction. In some situations, team members pressure others to "see things their way" and demonstrate their allegiance by joining particular camps and cliques. In order to facilitate this process, the person pits people against others through disrespectful and indirect communication.

VERBAL AND NON-VERBAL DYSFUNCTION

Dysfunctional communication often includes more than the specific words being used – it also incorporates how they are used. Thus, dysfunctional communication often includes veiled references, threats or "hints" (that only those involved would understand), pictures, un-funny humor, sarcastic "digs" and otherwise.

Further, dysfunctional communication can just as easily be non-verbal in nature, including eye-rolling, sighing loudly, smirking, avoiding eye contact, glaring, clenching of the fists, ignoring the person, turning one's back on someone, walking out of the room mid-sentence, shaking one's head in critical "disbelief" and repeatedly and persistently giving someone the silent treatment or cold shoulder.

Non-verbal dysfunction is as damaging as verbal dysfunction.

Simply put, comments such as "What's wrong with saying "*that*"?" or "I didn't say *a word*" often carry little weight in the diagnosis and assessment of workplace dysfunction.

ELECTRONIC COMMUNICATION AND SOCIAL MEDIA

Dysfunctional conduct and communication can take place off duty or on duty, yet still be captured by respectful workplace policies and safety and human rights legislation. The fundamental issue in each situation is the extent to which that communication or conduct is linked to dysfunction and disrespect at the workplace.

Social media, texting, e-mailing and other forms of electronic communication are prime examples of this. Many individuals irresponsibly engage in "computer courage" and post rude, defamatory, mean or generally disrespectful comments about their colleagues, leaders, clients, unions and employers. Commentary of this nature commonly constitutes dysfunctional behavior, regardless of when it is posted, sent or published, because of its impact on the day-to-day workplace environment.

To Re-cap

Well before leaders, consultants and other apparent "experts" in conflict management delve into "problem-solving," it is important to first and better understand the true nature of the problems that require the "solving."

- What are all of the potential Dots of dysfunction causing concern?

- Who are all the potential players/contributors to the dysfunction (directly or indirectly)?

- What are all of the potential dynamics at play (layoffs, significant change, operational restructuring)?

- How serious is the alleged dysfunction and how frequently does it arise?

- Where on the Scale of Dysfunctional Conduct might the various dysfunctional behaviors/practices fall?

Before rushing to scale down dysfunction, leaders must first learn more about the Scale of Dysfunctional Conduct and its significance as a critical diagnostic and remedial tool.

PART TWO

Peeling Away the Onion – Better Understanding the Many Layers of Workplace Dysfunction

I n Part One, we outlined the broad concepts that form the basis of a respectful and productive workplace. These concepts are important to understand – and apply – as they form the roots to success of any organizational approach to workplace respect. However, these foundational concepts are simply the start to gaining a full appreciation of workplace dynamics and, alone, they cannot effectively address issues surrounding dysfunctional behavior.

In fact, when organizations focus exclusively on the application of general concepts such as broad mission statements and general policies and procedures related to "acceptable" workplace behavior, communication and performance, they often end up creating more drama and dysfunction than they had set out to resolve.

Why is this the case?

When workplaces act on the basis of generalities, without fully understanding the specific qualities of the dysfunction at hand, they will fail to solve the actual workplace dynamics. In fact, in their attempts to implement a broad one-size-fits-all approach to unique and complex issues between individuals and among teams, organizations end up prolonging and complicating the sensitive situations at hand.

As time pressed as we all are, it is critical for leaders to take a moment to clearly understand and appreciate the many layers of dysfunctional team dynamics. This is what is addressed in Part Two.

First, we delve into a deeper understanding of the respective roles and responsibilities of those who engage in, observe or become aware of potentially dysfunctional interactions or behavior. Who, on the team, including leaders, might be considered as part of the dysfunction and in what way? Who, outside the team, also should be considered as potentially dysfunctional in the assessment and understanding of these dynamics?

Next, we consider who gets to decide what is and is not dysfunctional. As will be explained, it is not the most vocal or most common opinion that dictates whether a particular behavior, statement or interaction constitutes workplace dysfunction. Rather, dysfunction is defined using an objective test: the "Reasonable Person" test.

We then review the five most dysfunctional "personalities"

on a team. At least one, and sometimes more, shows up in environmental scans or workplace investigations regarding workplace dysfunction.

Finally, we evaluate the many "defenses" that are commonly put forth by those accused of engaging in dysfunctional or disruptive behavior. "Yes but ..." (with a list of excuses that follow) is how individuals commonly react when confronted with concerns about their behavior or performance. They attempt to justify or excuse their conduct by offering elaborate explanations for why they did what they did or said what they said. In this chapter, we will deconstruct those explanations to help readers understand the critical difference between *understanding* past behavior and *justifying* its continuation moving forward.

By the end of Part Two, readers will have a fulsome and rich understanding of the layers and complexities surrounding workplace dysfunction of all types. Armed with this knowledge, they will be in a prime position to resolve any dysfunction with which they are faced by applying the practical MIRROR Method outlined in Part Three.

Chapter 4

"WHO" MAY BE PART OF THE DYSFUNCTION?

Many workplace dramas are triggered by a complaint about "someone" doing "something" and a review is then conducted to determine if he/she "did it." This narrow approach may be suitable in situations involving discreet incidents of alleged workplace misconduct, such as theft, but does not work well to effectively understand, address or end interpersonal or team dysfunction.

DISSECTING THE LAYERS OF DISRESPECT

More often than not, there is more than one person involved in workplace dysfunction, each of whom contributes to the ongoing dynamics in different ways. To truly remedy this situation, leaders need to consistently ask three questions, regardless of who complains, what is reported, what is observed, or how a complaint is framed.

1. What is happening on this team?
2. What part of this is objectively dysfunctional?
3. Who is contributing to which part of the dysfunction?

Leaders must consider the potential contributing role of everyone, including the person who has come forward to complain, "innocent" bystanders, leaders and others (see Figure 6).

Figure 6
THE HUMANS BEHIND THE HOW

Consider this very simple scenario.

Mike and John are in a group meeting, waiting for Barb who is 10 minutes late. After they get started, Barb rushes in asking to be "caught up." Mike says, with humor tinged with sarcasm, "You snooze you lose – there is no replay button here." John laughs heartily.

Barb says, curtly, "Fine then ... just carry on."

After the meeting, Barb goes back to her team and relays what happened, including Mike's "rude and insensitive" comments to her. Mike hears about this and tells everyone that, once again, Barb is attempting to blame others for her inability to "show up" for the team.

Neither of them speaks to the other. Neither "clears the air."

From this point on, their relationship shifts slightly. They are cordial at best when with each other but then criticize each other to their colleagues. Over time, everyone has become aware of the fact that they don't get along and avoid each other.

MYTH: Leaders do not have to act until they receive a formal complaint, in writing, from a staff member.

REALITY: Leaders are expected to inquire into potential dysfunction as soon as they become aware of it, even if there is no formal or written complaint.

Their leader has heard about their strained relationship – from each of them – as well as others, yet is of the view they should figure out how to deal with each other. If they needed his help, they would have specifically asked. He acknowledges that each of them has mentioned the issue to him casually but neither has come forward with a "formal complaint," so he assumes they were just venting.

The Practical Realities of this Dysfunction

A traditional, historical way of approaching this scenario is to view Barb as the apparent "victim" of Mike's commentary, or to see this as an ongoing "personality difference" between Barb and Mike, with everyone else falling outside their drama and playing irrelevant roles.

However, in this day and age, both the legal and practical

realities demand that leaders take a systematic approach to understanding and resolving this dysfunction.

First, in many jurisdictions, and in a number of different workplace contexts (e.g., human rights, safety, negligence), the law expects that everyone involved in potentially problematic workplace dynamics or incidents play a role in rectifying them and mitigating the damage caused to specific individuals and the team as a whole. All individuals, including complainants, respondents, bystanders and leaders who are aware of or involved in the dysfunction, at any level, have some responsibility in addressing it.

Being aware of an issue – and failing to take steps to remedy or report it – will potentially result in individual and corporate liability for any resulting consequences, including prolonged damage caused by the continuing dysfunctional behavior.

Specifically:

- **Complainants**, such as Barb, are those individuals who perceive themselves to be the victim of someone else's inappropriate conduct/communication (such as Mike, who is commonly referenced as the "respondent," "defendant" or "accused"). Except in very serious situations (physical or sexual assault or harassment, for example), complainants are and should be expected to address their concerns with the respondent (with another person present for support if they so choose). If they are not comfortable speaking to the respondent at all, then, at minimum, they should report their concerns in a *confidential* manner to a frontline leader, manager or human resources professional. Once they have done so, they are expected to maintain confidentiality and refrain from attempting to influence the testimony or involvement of others. They also are expected not to engage in workplace vigilante justice, by taking matters into their own hands, responding to perceived disrespect by also engaging in disrespect or by building camps against the perceived perpetrator.

- **Respondents/accused/defendants** are those individuals who are accused of workplace disrespect, bullying, harassment or otherwise. They may or may not hold positions of leadership. Respondents (regardless of their perceived power, value or reputation in an organization) are expected to comply with all laws and policies related to professional and respectful workplace conduct. They also are expected to respect the confidential nature of the review processes and not attempt to influence the testimony or involvement of others nor can they in any way retaliate against those who have come forward.

- **Bystanders**, including and especially those in positions of leadership, are expected to intervene and shut down disrespectful conduct as soon as it is observed, whether or not the behavior relates to or is directed at someone on their team. At minimum, they should remove themselves from the situation as soon as they reasonably can and then report their observations to leadership or human resources to ensure the matter is addressed. It is no longer acceptable for bystanders – in any position in any organization – to say, "It doesn't involve me so it's not my problem."

- **Leaders,** who observe or become aware of potential dysfunction, must intervene in an objective and timely manner to inquire into the issues/concerns objectively, determine who is responsible for what aspects of the dysfunction (if any) and put an end to it through a comprehensive remedial plan. Leaders must act as soon as they become aware of a concern and cannot wait until they receive a formal complaint. Leaders are expected to look into and address all potential dysfunction in any situation, whether or not they have witnessed it, whether or not others have witnessed it and regardless of the fact that some or all of the individuals involved have refused to put their concerns in writing.

As the diagram in Figure 6 reflects, potential contributors to dysfunctional environments go beyond the narrow "team" and include individuals on other teams, in other organizations, members of the public, customers and others.

Practically speaking, if leaders take a narrow approach to their review of workplace dysfunction and focus only on a specific written or verbal complaint involving the complainant and the accused, they will mistakenly overlook a number of others who also may be furthering these or other contributing issues. They will assume they have found the *one* who is responsible for "the issue," only to find out later that the dysfunction has returned and worsened, perhaps looking a bit different but continuing to cause low engagement, high presenteeism and generalized malaise.

Thus, for both legal and practical reasons, it is incumbent on leaders to truly understand the nature and extent of all dysfunctional practices and dynamics on their teams before taking steps to remedy the situation.

Returning to the case scenario presented above, a thorough review of the workplace dysfunction, properly understood *might* result in one of these outcomes (depending on the specific evidence that turns up during the objective review).

- Barb may be held responsible for ongoing disruption arising from her punctuality and her failure to recognize how disrespectful it is to others when she persistently arrives at meetings late. Barb also might be responsible for speaking disrespectfully about Mike to other colleagues instead of addressing her concerns, in private, to Mike directly or to a frontline leader or someone in human resources.

- Mike might be held responsible for his sarcastic and negative commentary towards Barb during the meeting. While he may have had a legitimate concern regarding her lateness, it would have been respectful for him to have addressed this with Barb in private (instead of doing so in front of John) or, at minimum, without using sarcasm or personal "digs." Mike also may be responsible for ongoing team dysfunction and tension caused by him speaking disrespectfully about Barb to their colleagues (instead of using the confidential discreet venues available to him).

- John may be held responsible for laughing at Mike's commentary towards Barb (and therefore, contributing to the tension and dysfunction instead of working to shut it down and defuse it). He also could have suggested to Mike that they take their concerns to leadership together instead of using the informal avenues of gossip and backstabbing.

- Other colleagues may be considered bystanders, depending on the degree to which they were brought into the drama, by campaigning against and criticizing Barb and/or Mike. They, too, might be partially responsible for any critical conversations in which they participated (instead of shutting them down) and any potential failure to report the ongoing tension to leadership.

■ The leader is likely responsible for being aware of the negative dynamics between Barb and Mike and failing to properly inquire into and remedy these as soon as reasonably possible.

While the specifics of this particular dysfunction will only become evident after an investigation, that investigation will only be of genuine assistance to the health of this organization if it consistently asks "what is happening here?" and "who is responsible for what?"

Chapter 5

WHO GETS TO DIAGNOSE DYSFUNCTION?

Without question, "who" gets to decide what is or is not "dysfunctional" – and the basis upon which this decision is made – is commonly misunderstood and misapplied.

An Overview on What Matters – Feelings, Facts or Both?

Many individuals who see themselves as victims of dysfunction or recipients of offensive behavior believe that if they "feel" they have been treated disrespectfully, then this must be so. They think that they must simply report their experience, perceptions and feelings surrounding a negative workplace interaction in order for leaders to then take action and solve the problem.

At the same time, many individuals who see themselves as being unfairly accused of dysfunctional behavior believe that if, in their experience, they did not consider their comments or actions to be offensive and did not intend to act in a dysfunctional or disrespectful manner, then the concerns against them should be dismissed.

In both respects, individuals commonly and mistakenly assume that the determining factor in the diagnosis of disrespect and dysfunction is *subjective* experiences, intentions and responses to workplace dynamics.

This is not so. While it is important to consider individual perceptions, intentions and experiences, the ultimate diagnosis of any workplace dysfunction, including discrimination, harassment and bullying, is based on an objective assessment of the work environment.

MYTH: If the employee didn't intend to offend or disrespect others, then he/she shouldn't be held responsible.

REALITY: If the employee's conduct or communication is considered to be objectively offensive or dysfunctional, then it must be addressed. The lack of intention underlying the behavior is irrelevant.

This assessment takes place in two ways. First, an objective individual, who is not in any way involved in the particular dynamics, must consider the observations, perceptions and experiences of everyone involved as well as any other relevant information, and then determine what likely happened between or among the individuals involved. This aspect of the objective assessment will be elaborated upon later in the book, in Step 3 of the MIRROR Method, Conducting the Review.

Second, after determining what likely happened, the objective investigator must then ask how a "reasonable person" would view the overall circumstances; and, specifically, whether that reasonable person would consider the dynamics to be objectively dysfunctional in the current workplace.

The Reasonable Person Standard is based on the governing laws and organizational policies and procedures in effect at any given point in time. This standard for dysfunction does not change or vary from individual to individual on a team or from one workplace environment to another. Rather, it changes as the laws and policies change in relation to what is and is not acceptable workplace conduct, behavior and communication.

The Scale of Offensive Behavior

Figure 7

SCALE OF OFFENSIVE BEHAVIOR

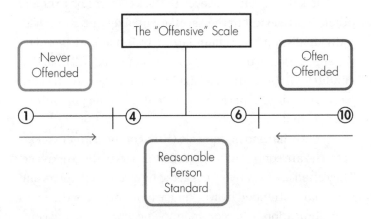

The Scale of Offensive Behavior (see Figure 7) illustrates these two different components of alleged workplace dysfunction – subjective and objective.

The horizontal scale shows the wide range of subjective perceptions and opinions in the workplace. The vertical scale shows the objective, Reasonable Person Standard, that governs the workplace, regardless of and despite individual opinions as to what is or is not dysfunctional, offensive or inappropriate.

UNDERSTANDING THE SUBJECTIVE EXPERIENCE OF DYSFUNCTION

At one end of the subjective scale (1 out of 10) are team members who are never offended. They often are unaware of and lack insight into their "objectively" offensive conduct because they do not see their conduct as offensive and often do not intend to be offensive to others. If it's not offensive to them, then it shouldn't be offensive to anyone else.

These individuals frequently react to complaints about their behavior with surprise, indicating that they had no intention to be disrespectful and had no desire to offend anyone.

Often, this is true. However, the lack of intention to offend others is irrelevant in the assessment of dysfunction. *If* an individual's conduct is found to be dysfunctional, based on the application of the Reasonable Person Standard, then that conduct will be defined as dysfunctional despite the subjective opinion, experience or intention of the person who engaged in it.

At the other end of the scale (10 out of 10) are team members who are commonly offended by others in the workplace. They often are negatively triggered by others' behaviors and personally offended by workplace dynamics, conduct and communication. They commonly expect behavior and communication to end if they personally view it as unacceptable or inappropriate. At times, they submit medical notes or lists of symptoms to support their reaction to their surroundings and interactions with others.

However, despite their genuine reactions to an incident or interaction at the workplace, if the behavior or communication in question is found not to be objectively dysfunctional/ offensive according to the Reasonable Person Standard then it will not be diagnosed or labeled as such, simply because one person reacted to it in a negative manner.

The Reasonable Person Standard is not only consistent with the law, it also makes sense practically. Workplaces are communal environments within which many different individuals work and interact. Each individual comes to the workplace with a different background and history. Each has his/her own beliefs, opinions and world views. An individual's subjective reaction to particular communication, incidents or interactions will be colored by this history. The subjective reaction also will vary depending on the individual's prior experience with and knowledge of those involved in the dysfunction, the topics being discussed and the overall context in which the behavior occurs.

Some individuals are personally more offended by certain incidents or comments than other individuals. Some individuals are more offended about certain topics than other topics. Some are more offended when sleep or food deprived.

Thus, subjective experiences and perceptions surrounding apparently disrespectful communication or offensive behavior will vary greatly both within an individual and between individuals. It would be chaotic and inherently unfair to base a finding or diagnosis of dysfunction (which often leads to serious consequences for those found to have engaged in dysfunction) on a moving and highly variable target of an individual's subjective experience.

While it is important to be considerate and mindful of each person's experiences in the workplace, a determination as to whether that experience is, in fact, dysfunctional has to be based on an objective standard.

THE NOTION OF THE "REASONABLE PERSON"

The vertical line on the Scale (see Figure 7) reflects the Reasonable Person Standard. As set out above, the reasonable person is not necessarily the person who has come forward to report the concern or the person who is defending his/her behavior. Rather, the reasonable person is based on the notional reasonable person who is knowledgeable of and acts in compliance with current laws, policies and procedures surrounding acceptable workplace communication and conduct.

The Reasonable Person Standard does not change depending on the industry, profession, education, experience or generation involved in the alleged dysfunction. The standard only changes as the laws, legislation and societal expectations change in relation to appropriate workplace behavior.

In applying the Reasonable Person Standard to the assessment of workplace dysfunction, it is important to ask questions such as:

- Would a reasonable person in the complainant's position have viewed or experienced the alleged behavior, communication or interaction as unreasonably offensive/harassing/intimidating?

- Would a reasonable person in the accused's position have understood or anticipated that his/her behavior might be seen or experienced as unreasonably offensive/harassing/intimidating?

If, in applying this test, the behavior meets the Reasonable Person Standard then it should not be considered objectively dysfunctional and should not result in an adverse or punitive response towards the individual who engaged in it, regardless of the complainant's subjective reaction to the situation.

However, if in applying this test, the behavior fails to meet the Reasonable Person Standard, then the behavior should be considered objectively dysfunctional and the person who engaged in this conduct should be held accountable for it, regardless of his/her lack of intention, malice or otherwise.

The Scale of Offensive Behavior and Negotiated Relationships

While it is important to understand the distinction between the subjective experiences and objective realities surrounding the definition of workplace dysfunction, in practice, many workplaces allow for the presence of communication and conduct that may fall below or exceed the Reasonable Person Standard. This happens, over time, through individuals developing clear boundaries and negotiating individualized personal relationships with each other.

As one example, two individuals may be at 1 or 2 on the Scale of Offensive Behavior, either generally or when it comes to working with each other. Over the years, they may have developed a relationship in which their conduct or communication may not meet the objective Reasonable Person Standard but does not offend either of them. As long as their 1-2 conduct with each other does not offend others who are situated in the same area at the time, then it is often not an issue.

In contrast, there may be a team that includes an individual at 8 or 9 on the Scale. Over the years, the team has become aware of ways in which this individual is triggered in the workplace. This might include environmental triggers, such as the playing of radios or social chit-chat. Or, it might include certain types of interactions, body contact or references that, while not objectively unreasonable, create personal discomfort for the individual involved.

In a negotiated relationship, the team respects these triggers, and *reasonably* attempts to minimize such triggers in the presence of that individual, despite the fact that some of the communication or behaviors that caused this person to react would not be seen as "objectively offensive" using the legal standard of a reasonable person. They do this in the name of workplace harmony and team building. In these circumstances, the person at 8-9 must realize (or be told) that others are customizing their communication or behavior in relation to him/her specifically, out of respect for his/her personal triggers, circumstances and desires. That person must not expect this customized, negotiated relationship to be applied to redefine the general Reasonable Person Standard for the overall workplace.

MYTH: If someone feels bullied, it means they are being bullied. If someone feels offended, it means the other person was offensive.

REALITY: If someone feels bullied, the leader needs to inquire into the situation by having the individual provide particulars about the perceived bullying. The leader then needs to apply the MIRROR Method to assess those concerns objectively.

The Clash Between Negotiated Relationships and the Reasonable Person Standard

Often, an individual will assert that he/she was in a negotiated relationship with the person who has raised the concerns and, as a result, it was reasonable for him/her to think that the conduct or communication would be seen as acceptable by that individual. The existence of a negotiated relationship between individuals is a question of fact. The person who makes this assertion (that is, that there was a negotiated relationship) must prove – objectively – that this was the case (by presenting information, such as e-mails or discussions, that informed his/her belief that a negotiated relationship existed). If the person cannot prove the presence of a negotiated relationship, then his/her conduct or behavior will be judged in accordance with the governing, objective Reasonable Person Standard.

In summary, while it is important to be cognizant of individuals' opinions and preferences in the workplace, the ultimate determination as to whether particular communication or conduct is dysfunctional is objective in nature. The communication of one's boundaries and subjective degree of "offense" is critical to the building of negotiated relationships but does not dictate the formal determination of workplace dysfunction.

Chapter 6

THE FIVE MOST COMMON DYSFUNCTIONS OF INDIVIDUALS

As legal counsel and a third-party, neutral investigator and mediator, I have been involved in hundreds of workplace reviews, investigations and other formal processes involving serious workplace "incidents," long-standing interpersonal drama and dysfunction and significant and systemic team breakdowns. Not surprisingly, I am often called in at the point of no return (that is, at the "train wreck"). Serious incidents have happened, formal complaints have been filed, engagement scores have dropped significantly and the rate of turnover and absenteeism is unmanageable.

I have reviewed dysfunctional practices in the private and public sectors, involving men and women, of various ages, ethnicities, educational levels, professional designations and otherwise.

I can say, without hesitation, that teams with significant and prolonged workplace dysfunction contain at least one and often more of the following five "dysfunctional" personalities.

Aggressive Andy

Aggressive Andy ("AA") is described as consistently showing up at work in an aggressive and overbearing way. AA takes over meetings, demands that certain work be assigned to him/her and sabotages any processes, decisions or changes with which he/she disagrees. AA is intimidating to staff and insubordinate to leaders.

MYTH: AA is simply passionate about the issue at hand.

REALITY: There is a distinction between being passionate and engaging in dysfunctional conduct. Individuals should be encouraged to communicate their concerns or ideas. Respectful workplaces do not stifle those who are driven to make positive change or raise genuine issues of concern. However, this "drive" or "passion" for change will not justify engaging in dysfunctional conduct in the name of such change, such as intimidating or silencing those with diverse views, co-opting discussions or personalizing professional disagreements.

Staff commonly attribute the following phrases to AA in their workplaces.

- "It's my way or the highway."
- "Your ideas don't matter."
- "If I wanted your opinion, I would have asked for it."
- "This is how we do things around here."
- "I am the Boss. If you wanted to make decisions, you should have applied for my position so do what I say."

In meetings, AA often talks over others, interrupts others and uses disrespectful body language (e.g., eye rolling, smirking, laughing, turning away, texting) to purposely silence, dismiss or discount the opinions of others.

When individuals disagree with AA's views or suggestions, they are too intimidated to say anything because of the negative and caustic fallout.

AA commonly personalizes and prolongs any "challenge" to his/her viewpoints by isolating and shunning those individuals who question AA's opinions. AA takes "professional disagreements" outside the boardroom and into the lunchroom – by ignoring and dismissing anyone who he/she has categorized as "unsupportive."

Over time, AA creates a culture in which others "give up" and simply go through the motions instead of dealing with the ugly aftermath associated with speaking up. People who can leave, do, and people who can't, keep their heads down and do as they are told.

At best, this creates a culture of mediocrity. The status quo is never questioned and the team continues to operate in a certain way only because this is the way in which they always have operated. There is a significant reluctance to question what is happening, let alone suggest trying something different.

At worst, this creates a culture of fear. Individuals who are aware of unsafe, unethical or questionable practices are too fearful to step up and say anything for fear of repercussions from AA (and his/her allies). In most serious/systemic cases of bullying/harassment, safety violations, financial misappropriation and otherwise, many individuals (from frontline staff to senior executives) were aware of potential violations yet were too scared to come forward. Those who had attempted to come forward commonly describe the many ways in which their concerns were silenced or dismissed and how aggressively they were "discouraged" from speaking about it further.

Moody Morgan

Moody Morgan ("MM") is, as the name suggests, moody and unpredictable. MM has "good days" (which are disappointingly infrequent) and "bad days" (which are dreaded by those around him/her). Team members vigilantly monitor MM's verbal and non-verbal behavior, at the outset of the day/shift to determine what kind of day MM is having as this will largely determine the kind of day the rest of the team will be having as well.

MYTH: Everyone has their good days and bad days.

REALITY: While everyone's moods are variable, not everyone holds others captive to their moods. Knowingly or not, MM's moods (good or bad) infiltrate the overall environment. If MM has a bad day, so does everyone else. This is not acceptable. Each of us must regulate our moods/behavior to ensure that others are treated with respect and civility.

On MM's bad days, he/she is often unresponsive, sulky and disengaged. When MM does communicate, it will be on MM's terms and timeline regardless of the operational needs of others or the organization at large. The communication itself is cringe-worthy. MM is impatient, curt, negative and uncooperative.

As soon as others recognize that MM is having a bad day, they attempt to avoid him/her at all costs. Some have the luxury of doing so, while others have to deal with it and hope for the best.

On MM's good days, he/she is everything he/she isn't during the bad days. MM bounces into the workplace, with positivity and enthusiasm, and attempts to engage with colleagues (and staff, if MM is the leader). MM becomes hurt and confused when those around him/her are not receptive or welcoming and often wonders what is wrong with them.

The unpredictability associated with MM is described as "exhausting." Team members rush to get as much done as possible on MM's good days, so they can restrict the amount of time they have to spend with MM on his/her bad days. It is MM's moods – rather than the needs of the operation – that seem to dictate what is happening and when.

Staff commonly describe working with MM as "walking on eggshells" because "they simply do not know which M is coming to work that day."

Perfectionist Pat

Perfectionist Pat ("PP") sets a high standard for him/herself and others, which PP consistently meets and often exceeds. From a performance perspective, PP is commonly a top producer in both quantity and quality. PP comes in early, leaves late and never misses a day of work. On the face of it, PP truly does look "perfect."

However, despite these achievements, PP often is one of the most disruptive team members, a fact that, perhaps conveniently, is unrecognized and left unaddressed by the leaders of the team.

How is PP disruptive? First, the standard set by PP is PP's standard, not that of the organization or workplace leader. It often is higher than what is expected by others and, usually, different in substance. However, because PP achieves this standard, and adds significant value to the end product, PP takes it upon him/herself to constantly monitor, evaluate, question and comment on the attendance and performance of others.

MYTH: It is important to ensure that others do their work properly.

REALITY: It is leadership's responsibility to ensure employees meet the expectations of their position as defined by the standards of the organization. Often, there are many ways to perform work – the fact that one individual's approach differs from another's does not mean that he/she is performing work "improperly." This needs to be assessed and addressed by the leaders. Colleagues should not be imposing their standards on other team members.

Specifically, PP commonly asks about others' workloads, absences from work, medical appointments, start times, break times, early departures, deadlines and completion of specific tasks. Sometimes, PP approaches colleagues directly to question them or give them unsolicited critical feedback about their work. Sometimes, PP talks about colleagues' "weaknesses" to others, including team members, clients and other individuals both within and outside the organization. Sometimes, PP approaches leaders to complain about his/her colleagues and provide unsolicited suggestions on how those leaders can and should be addressing these issues. PP often is as critical of leadership as he/she is of other team members.

In demanding perfection in themselves and others, PPs create a divisive, unsettling team environment. Team members do not trust PP to support them as he/she is constantly complaining about their work. Rather than being a go-to person or mentor, the team avoids and fears PP because of his/her attitude of superiority and unrelenting criticism. Instead of being the person to seek out for help, PP is the person most avoided.

PPs are not in leadership positions and should not make it "their job" to oversee productivity and performance. Their own success should not provide them with a foundation on which to criticize, demean or belittle others. If PPs wish to play an oversight role, they need to secure a position within leadership. Until then, they need to focus on their own work, not on others.

Negative Nic

Negative Nic ("NN") is commonly found on teams having low morale, significant disengagement and high turnover. NN is a glass-half-empty person who seems to be habitually focused on the negative aspects of the workplace and society in general. On a daily basis, NN will complain about what is wrong at work, at home and otherwise.

NN is not a critical thinker who has concerns with specific issues, raises them in the proper forum and presents possible solutions to consider. No, NN complains just to complain. It is as if complaining and negativity is habitually soothing to NN, while being simultaneously disruptive to others.

Team members describe NN's behavior as "exhausting" and "energy/soul sucking." Team members avoid asking NN how he/she is or inviting NN to participate in discussions (social or work-related), because they know that NN will complain about everything and anything. On team projects, NN is constantly playing devil's advocate and pointing out what won't work, without suggesting what might.

Uncontrolled negativity is powerful and contagious. Over time, NNs create a culture of negativity. If there are more NNs than not, the team becomes negative and stops working productively. In many workplaces, there is a "camp" of NNs who heavily influence the energy and effectiveness of the team as a whole. If not managed early and effectively, NNs can create a systemic epidemic that is difficult to fix.

Terry the Triangulator

Terry the Triangulator ("TT") often combines the destructive traits of others (the negativity of NN, the aggressiveness of AA, the need to interfere by PP and the unpredictability of MM) to create destructive triangulation on teams. Through divisive gossip and the improper and inaccurate relaying of information, rooted in a significant desire to control others, TT pits team members against each other and destroys trust and communication in the workplace.

TTs at the leadership level improperly share confidential information provided by one employee about another or confidential information about one employee with others. TTs also are known to survey staff about each other in a dysfunctional and divisive manner.

MYTH: Individuals who convey to one team member what others are saying about him/her are simply trying to make things better.

REALITY: Commonly, TTs preface their communication of workplace gossip by saying "I am doing this for your own good" (or "for the good of the team"). However, passing on hurtful information serves no useful purpose. If TTs wish to improve workplace dynamics, they should stop the malicious commentary and gossip as soon as it happens or report it to a leader so that it can be reviewed properly. They should not "stir up trouble" by simply passing the message on to the subject of the gossip as a heads-up.

TTs who are team members unnecessarily share half-truths, spin stories and gossip about one colleague with others. Usually, the information is shared to incite conflict and build distrust. Those who hear TT's stories stop trusting each other, which usually results in a significant team breakdown.

Unlike the behaviors of the other four, TT is commonly strategic and deliberate in his/her actions. This has serious ramifications on the health, strength and credibility of the team. Many staff leave when they can while others leave when they have to, usually by having to take sick leave.

Importantly, many times, dysfunctional teams have more than one dysfunction on the team. Also, one individual may manifest more than one of these dysfunctional behaviors.

Finally, it is common for teams to have two different types of the same form of dysfunction. For example, one AA might be an employee with significant seniority and experience who asserts that the long-standing practices are tried and true and make the most sense for the workplace in question. On the same team, there might be another AA, who is a new graduate and academic scholar who is insistent that the old school is failing to follow defensible best practices. It is not the views of either AA that cause the turmoil on their teams. Rather, it is the overbearing and controlling way in which each may be expressing or advocating a particular position.

It is critical for leaders to be aware of these types of dysfunctions given their prevalence in fractured team environments. However, each situation always needs to be assessed uniquely and objectively, based on a comprehensive and contextual evaluation of the specific ways in which AA, MM, PP, NN, or TT operate and whether those practices are unreasonable and unreasonably interfering with others on the team.

Chapter 7

INEXCUSABLE "EXCUSES" FOR WORKPLACE DYSFUNCTION

In order to understand and effectively remedy workplace dysfunction, leaders need to be aware of the distinction between *understanding* what has triggered, contributed or led to dysfunctional behavior and *justifying* or *excusing* the behavior itself.

The "Why" Does Not Justify the "How"

Often, in response to concerns about unacceptable behavior, performance or communication, individuals will "defend" their behavior by putting forth a variety of excuses and explanations. That is, an individual will admit to engaging in some or all of the poor performance or conduct but then offer an excuse or explanation for engaging in it. "I said or did that, but here's why...."

It is appropriate for individuals to provide a thorough response and *explanation* for their role in alleged dysfunctional conduct. However, it is not acceptable or appropriate for them to use this explanation as a justification or excuse for objectively dysfunctional, unacceptable workplace behavior, communication or performance. Another way of saying this is that the Whys (the underlying reasons for behavior) will never justify the Hows (the dysfunctional nature of their behavior or performance).

Figure 8
THE WHY DOES NOT JUSTIFY THE HOW

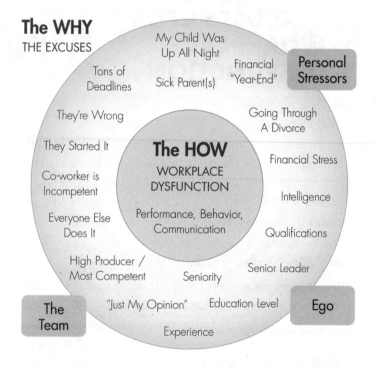

There are many different Whys. Some tug at leaders' heartstrings and cause them to feel guilty for holding an individual accountable for dysfunctional behavior. Others, particularly those tied to an individual's apparent influence within the organization, intimidate leaders and create significant pressure on them to remain willfully blind to dysfunctional behavior, despite its significant and adverse impact on the overall team or organization.

Unquestionably, it is important to understand why individuals are behaving or performing in a certain manner and then actively help them to change their unacceptable behavior or performance. This might include training, counseling, medical accommodations, paid or unpaid leaves, adjustments to their workplace environment/work space and otherwise. What it cannot include is allowing unacceptable behavior or performance to continue. That is not support – that is enablement.

THE PERSONAL WHYS – IT'S ALL ABOUT ME

The first category of Whys are the personal reasons put forth to explain unacceptable workplace performance, behavior or communication.

Everyone, at one point or another, encounters difficulties in their lives – family illness, personal illness, financial hardship and relationship breakdowns to name but a few. Many individuals also experience personal stressors at work – financial year-end, strategic planning, budgetary restraints, staffing challenges, intense workload and so on. However, only a small proportion of individuals use these circumstances to justify performing poorly (on a consistent basis) or being rude, dismissive, angry or unresponsive to those with whom they work.

Similarly, many individuals point to their unique personalities as personal Whys, such as "I'm moody; I'm outspoken; I'm passionate; I'm not a morning person." Again, a number of individuals have fluctuating moods, feel strongly about certain issues, operate better at certain times of the day than others and prefer being direct. However, most have learned to regulate their moods and customize their messaging and conduct in a manner that is civil and respectful.

The only difference between those who rely on personal Whys and those who don't is the attempt to use their personal experiences, situations, attributes or preferences to justify why they should be treated differently from everyone else in the workplace.

MYTH: Staff or leaders who are "stressed out" need to be given "space" to sort out their issues.

REALITY: Everyone has competing personal and professional challenges. While it is important to support individuals through their specific issues, this should not happen at the expense of the work environment. People can be given "space" as long as they continue to be respectful and responsive to others on work-related matters. Their issues cannot be used as an excuse to treat others poorly or to justify their abdication of work responsibilities.

As sad, legitimate or understandable as a personal Why might sound or be, it does not and will not justify how that person performs at work or interacts with others. No personal experience – at work or at home – and no personality trait, personal history or background can be used to justify unacceptable, disrespectful and dysfunctional workplace behavior.

THE WORK WHYS – IT'S ALL ABOUT THEM

The second category of Whys is team-based and rooted in the behaviors of or dynamics involving others or the overall organizational culture. Using this Why, individuals often point to similar behavior of other team members as justification for their conduct. Or, they rely on historical condonation of their behavior by previous leadership.

Commonly they will say, "This is exactly what so and so does" or "This is how we have always done things around here."

Alternatively, they justify their own unacceptable behavior by highlighting another person's dysfunction on the team. They commonly say, "If that person showed up and did their work properly, like the rest of us, there would be no need to mouth off at them."

Finally, they will often rely on operational dynamics, such as unreasonable workload, excessive overtime, staffing issues, reduced budgets, cramped conditions and otherwise to justify their behavioral outbursts or poor performance.

None of these explanations, however accurate or legitimate, act as an excuse to justify ongoing and unacceptable workplace behavior or practices.

THE WHYS OF WHO – DON'T YOU KNOW WHO I AM?

The third common category of Whys is rooted in "Who" is performing or acting in an unacceptable, disruptive/dysfunctional manner. In this category, individuals (and organizations) attempt to justify clearly dysfunctional behavior on the basis of their position, status or perceived value or threat to the organization. These Whys include:

- He is the CEO.
- She is the Union President.
- He has been here for 25 years.
- She has two PhDs.
- He is our top sales guy.

- She files multiple lawsuits.
- He constantly goes to the media.
- She is our only employee in the region.
- He will retire within the year.

With each of these Whys, the focus is not on the dysfunctional behavior or its adverse effects on others but, rather, on the "identity" of the person engaged in the behavior and the potential consequences to the leader or organization if that person reacts poorly to being held accountable (by leaving, litigating or otherwise).

The Why related to the Who is not a respectful, reasonable or legally defensible basis on which to ignore dysfunctional/disruptive behavior. There is one standard of civility, respect and communication that has to be met by everyone in the workplace regardless of their position within the organization, years of experience/seniority, technical skills and abilities, type of educational degree or degree of fear they have instilled in those around them.

Understanding Versus Justifying the "Why" – The Need for Support, Not Enablement

As stated above, while the Why that underlies or contributes to someone's behavior cannot be used to excuse or justify poor performance or disrespectful conduct towards others, it often cannot be ignored completely, particularly when it comes to an individual's personal or familial illness or systemic, contributing challenges within the workplace generally.

SUPPORTING PERSONAL WHYS

If someone is going through a personal crisis, such as a relationship breakdown or financial crisis, it is important for leaders to *understand* how those circumstances are contributing to the workplace issues. This information is not considered in order to justify why the ongoing dysfunction should continue, but rather, to assist the leader in supporting individuals to make the necessary changes to their behavior or performance. Support in these circumstances may include paid or unpaid leaves, adjustments to work assignments or workloads and otherwise.

The most significant Why put forward by individuals often relates to a medical condition from which they might suffer. If dysfunctional behavior is triggered by an underlying mental or physical disability, then, in many jurisdictions, organizations have a legal duty to accommodate that disability *to the point of undue hardship*.

This does *not* mean that leaders can or should excuse consistently unacceptable performance or disruptive behavior or allow it to continue to the detriment of others at the workplace; it means that they should work with the individual and qualified medical experts to devise a supportive and balanced plan that effectively addresses this disruptive behavior while at the same time providing support to the individual.

For example, an individual who has repeated vocal outbursts towards his colleagues may assert that he suffers from diabetes and it is because of this condition that he yells and loses his temper. If the condition of diabetes and associated symptoms are objectively established, then the organization needs to support this individual by establishing a plan to address those symptoms that have an adverse effect on the workplace environment.

While each accommodation plan must be designed on an individualized basis, past examples have included clearly defined and regularly scheduled meal breaks, early intervention and behavioral management strategies for regulating moods/communication and ensuring compliance with a medical treatment plan that is regularly reviewed and updated.

The organization must ensure that while support is offered to the individual in question by implementing accommodation plans, the ongoing aggressive, disruptive conduct is not allowed to continue in the name of the underlying condition. That is, the individual should be supported through the accommodation plan but the unacceptable behavior should not be allowed to continue at the expense of others in the workplace.

SUPPORTING WORK WHYS

Where the underlying explanations involve workplace/systemic challenges (including the behavior or performance of other individuals), the employer can support the individual by making all reasonable efforts to consider and address these concerns.

For example, in response to concerns regarding workload or overtime fatigue, leaders can review the distribution of workload, scheduling and staffing resources. In response to concerns about others engaging in similar or different types of dysfunction, such as poor performance, safety infractions or disruptive or disrespectful behavior, leaders should objectively and independently review these matters, confidentially, through the MIRROR Method.

If the organizational culture has condoned disrespect, then leadership needs to reset the organizational hard drive, establish new expectations for the entire team and begin to hold everyone accountable on the basis of the revised and updated expectations.

In holding individuals accountable for their unacceptable behavior or performance and at the same time being aware of and responsive to the underlying triggers for that behavior/performance, organizations increase the likelihood of truly preventing and/or resolving the many aspects of workplace dysfunction in a sustainable and systemic manner.

NO SUPPORT FOR THE WHYS OF WHO

Simply put, there is no way in which to properly support an individual's efforts to justify – or avoid personal responsibility for – unacceptable performance or behavior based on his/her identity or status within an organization. Without question, individuals need to be appreciated and reinforced for the value they bring to an organization (through increased profits, enhanced profile or otherwise). However, that value does not displace the obligation to behave and communicate with others in a respectful and civilized manner.

PART THREE

So There MIGHT be Dysfunction: NOW What?

I n the first half of this book we spent the necessary time sorting out "workplace dysfunction" at a theoretical and conceptual level. This is important because, before taking action, it is necessary to fully understand what needs to be acted upon and why.

However, too many leadership models focus exclusively on analyzing the problem of workplace dysfunction and emphasizing that something must be done. They do not, however, explain exactly what that something is or how it should happen. This leaves many leaders feeling frustrated and disempowered. Often, they are aware that a situation is developing and know, at some level, that they should respond. The vexing issue they most commonly face is *how* to do so. That is, how do they properly, fairly and defensibly review and address disruptive, disrespectful and dysfunctional behavior?

The second half of this book provides the answers to this question. It outlines a straightforward six-step process, the MIRROR Method, for leaders – at all levels of any organization – to follow in order to effectively monitor, accurately review, diagnose and successfully remedy workplace dysfunction. It shows leaders how to fairly and objectively hold individuals accountable for unacceptable workplace behavior, communication and performance so that the entire team can work productively in a safe and respectful environment.

Why Is it Called the MIRROR Method?

In my work, I use a mirror as an analogy to address many aspects of workplace dysfunction. To me, mirrors are a rich metaphorical tool to use to "see" what is going on – in us, in others and on our teams generally.

First, *self-reflection* – on the part of everyone involved, including leaders – is critical to successful resolution of any workplace dysfunction. Individuals need to ask themselves how they are "showing up" at the workplace and how they may be contributing to the dysfunctional situation, perhaps inadvertently. It is not enough – or appropriate – to repeatedly complain about what others are doing to cause the dysfunction. Teams will only be successful if each individual, including the leader, reflects on whether their communication or conduct is making the situation better or worse. This includes not only what they are saying and doing but *how*.

Second, when triggered by others' behavior or performance in the workplace, it is important to "mirror" back to them how their behavior is being perceived and how it is affecting the overall environment. This should happen soon after the disruptive behavior or performance has begun, in order to facilitate early, respectful and effective workplace change.

In many situations, individuals wrongly assume that those who perform or behave inappropriately are:

1. aware of what they are doing and how they are "showing up;" and

2. are doing it on purpose, with the intent of causing harm to others.

Rarely are these assumptions true.

In fact, in our time-crunched and high-pressured world, team members (including leaders themselves) are busy meeting work and home demands and often are not aware of how they are showing up at the workplace or how their communication or conduct is affecting those around them.

The first step in building workplace respect is to let others know about the concerns surrounding their behavior by clearly "mirroring" to them how they are being seen in the workplace and how they are affecting others. Legally and ethically, individuals deserve to be given this feedback explicitly, clearly and neutrally before being expected to change. The MIRROR conversation, set out in the MIRROR Method (and referenced previously in Chapter 3, Understanding the Scope of Dysfunction: Is It a "Bad Day" or a "Bad Life"), provides a way to facilitate this necessary dialogue in a constructive and practical manner.

Finally, as leaders, it is important to regularly reflect on how the overall team is functioning by taking stock of various criteria – individual conduct, interpersonal dynamics, operational metrics and systemic patterns. At an individual level, are there staff who are not behaving in an acceptable or respectful manner? Interpersonally, are there particular individuals who are not working well together, at the expense of overall team harmony, productivity and efficiency? At an operational level, are there staff who are not attending work regularly or performing at a level expected of them (in terms of accuracy, productivity or otherwise)? At a systemic level, is there notable turnover or a significant issue with sick leave on a particular team or in a specific department?

The MIRROR Method emphasizes the importance of ongoing and accurate *reflection* of the dynamics at all levels of any organization as the first and critical step towards the detection and elimination of workplace dysfunction.

MYTH: Individuals must be aware of how they come across to others on the team.

REALITY: More often than not, individuals who engage in dysfunctional conduct are focused on their own personal and professional schedules and stressors and do not see themselves in the same way as others see them. It is important to respectfully let them know how their specific behaviors/communication practices are affecting particular individuals or the team in general.

Brief Summary of the MIRROR Method

Using reflection as its foundation, the MIRROR Method provides all leaders (including unionized frontline supervisors, managers and CEOs) with a basic six-step process to use to address dysfunction at any level of the organization. This process can and should be customized to any size and type of team and to any type of dysfunction with which it is faced, from minor to significant, from performance to behavior to communication.

The MIRROR Method shows leaders how to accurately monitor for and detect potential dysfunction in individuals or among the team generally. It also guides leaders on how to *objectively* and defensibly assess the nature, extent and legitimacy of "apparent" or reported dysfunction on the team and then design a substantive and comprehensive response to any dysfunction that has been confirmed through an objective review.

In brief, the six steps of the MIRROR Method are:

M – MONITOR the workplace for potential signs and symptoms of dysfunction;

I – INQUIRE into the nature and extent of the potential dysfunction, using the MIRROR Triage Process, in order to determine the type of workplace review to conduct;

R – REVIEW the alleged dysfunction objectively, using an informal or formal process (based on the results of the Triage Process);

R – REMEDY the individual dysfunction in accordance with the results of the objective review, using a combination of accountability and support;

O – OPERATIONALLY restore trust, communication and credibility among the team as a whole; and

R – REVISIT the "scene" of the dysfunction to determine whether the remedial and restorative processes were successful.

The MIRROR Method constitutes a systematic and defensible process in which to objectively review and address any dysfunction in the workplace, from general observations of the leader to informal concerns of coworkers to formal complaints, grievances or litigation.

No leader can guarantee that their response to workplace dysfunction will go unchallenged or be successful in changing someone else's behavior or performance. However, in following the MIRROR Method, leaders will be able to defend the steps they took, efforts they made and decisions they reached, both in how they were made and the manner in which they were implemented. This will go a long way in enhancing their credibility as leaders both within and outside their organization.

Key Tips for the MIRROR Method

Here are some guiding principles that apply to each step of the MIRROR Method.

1. **Consistency:** It is important for leaders to follow the MIRROR Method consistently. All allegations of workplace dysfunction should be reviewed and remedied using the MIRROR Method, regardless of the particular team member (or team) involved. The MIRROR Method is a comprehensive and defensible method of holding individuals and teams accountable. However, it will quickly become indefensible if the method is applied "differently" to different members of the same team, to different teams within the same organization or if it is only applied to some team members and not others.

Inconsistent accountability, in the face of similar behaviors or performance, is rarely defensible, regardless of how "clean" the process may appear to be. Staff actively monitor for and are keenly aware of differential treatment, particularly when it comes to workplace dysfunction and performance management. Inconsistency by leaders, in the use and application of the MIRROR Method, will reduce the effectiveness of the process and result in significant concerns surrounding the credibility and trust of the leader involved.

2. **"Brown Bagging" It:** In order to ensure that the MIRROR Method is followed in a fair and consistent manner, leaders should ensure they can pass the "Brown Bag" test. This is a test of consistent leadership and personal self-reflection to use in the implementation of the process itself.

When inquiring into or reviewing a workplace concern, what if those involved (that is, those who reported the concern and those being reported) all had *brown bags* over their heads? Would the leader's response or reaction to the particular allegations or concerns change once the bags were removed and the identities of the persons revealed?

When determining a remedy, how would the leader respond to the situation, based on the findings and conclusions uncovered by an objective review, if they were unaware of the identities of those involved?

To ensure the consistent and fair application of the MIRROR Method, the identities of those involved should be irrelevant in terms of the process being followed or outcome being implemented. If certain concerns are ignored, certain reviews are cursory or certain allegations are disproportionately and aggressively investigated based solely on the identities of those involved, there is a strong indication of potential bias – real or perceived – on the part of the leader. This will undercut the objectivity and credibility of the entire MIRROR Method regardless of how "fair" the process might appear to be.

3. **Documentation:** It is not enough to simply follow the steps of the MIRROR Method in a consistent manner; it is critical to establish and record that this has been done.

In recent complaints against leadership in the context of workplace dysfunction, the focus has expanded from "they have ignored dysfunction" to "they took far too long to address it."

Accordingly, it is important for leaders to document in writing, concurrently and in chronological order, the steps they have taken in relation to the MIRROR Method.

The Process Timeline is a tool that facilitates documentation by leaders regarding the efforts they have made to effect positive changes in individuals through implementation of the MIRROR Method. It should include the timing and type of scheduled intervention, such as interviews and meetings, any canceled meetings (by the employee, leader or otherwise) and the reasons for such cancellation, any requests for documentation, delays in receiving this documentation and reasons for the delay.

The Process Timeline will reflect how the MIRROR Method unfolded and outline the particular individuals and circumstances responsible for any delays.

Figure 9
PROCESS TIMELINE

Employee Name:		
Date	**Event** (meeting, communication with employee, cancellations, timelines, goals, coaching)	**Follow-up /** **Action Completed**

4. It's How You Do It: Ultimately, in applying the MIRROR Method, it is important for leaders to consider not only whether they are following the MIRROR Method in a timely manner, but *how* they are doing so. This includes how they are speaking to, communicating about and generally treating those who are involved.

5. Show them How It's Done: When implementing the MIRROR Method, it is important for leaders to be respectful, compassionate and transparent in their interactions with those involved because of apparent concerns with their behavior or performance. The old school yet far too common leadership practices of withholding information, gossiping about, yelling at, shunning, shaming, humiliating or belittling individuals being investigated or performance managed has no place in the modern workplace – legally, ethically or otherwise.

6. Discipline with a Whisper: Leaders are expected to be role models when it comes to respectful and acceptable workplace behavior and communication. The fact that a staff member is being investigated or held accountable through the MIRROR Method, regardless of how serious the dysfunction might be, does not give any leader a reasonable or defensible basis to depart from expected norms regarding respect and civility in the workplace.

Some leaders argue that they need to get their point across – using persuasive "force" if necessary – in order to be heard. They use non-verbal "disapproving" facial expressions (sighing, rolling of the eyes, grimacing), a stern tone of voice or other body language (shaking of their head, pointing at the person, "slapping" their hand on the desk) to demonstrate that they are displeased with the individual's behavior or explanation for that behavior. They also may socially retreat from or isolate the person being addressed by limiting any day-to-day interactions or discussions with that employee. In extreme situations, they encourage others to do the same.

This type of reaction, regardless of the motivation, will not assist the leader in achieving a successful outcome; in fact, it often results in further difficulties and complications. Leaders who use the MIRROR Method in a disrespectful manner will expose themselves to complaints of harassment and bullying for the *manner* in which they have implemented the process. The fact that one of their team members may be engaged in poor performance, unacceptable behavior or serious misconduct will not be a defense to the leader's disrespect towards them while investigating or responding to these concerns.

This response is not only indefensible, it is unnecessary in order to achieve a successful outcome with the MIRROR Method. If leaders apply steps of the MIRROR Method consistently and diligently, they will be able to effectively eliminate dysfunctional workplace behavior and performance without needing to resort to disrespectful behavior in doing so.

I commonly remark that successful leaders who effectively use the MIRROR Method can "discipline with a whisper." That is, leaders can use the tools in the MIRROR Method to clearly communicate their expectations and create necessary change without using unacceptable leadership practices to do so. *Tough* decisions should not be made in a *rough* manner.

The MIRROR Method, particularly the section on Remedy (Step 4), provides leaders with concrete ways in which to hold individuals accountable through communication, documentation and escalation. Defensible leadership is established through proper and respectful application of these principles – in conjunction with all other steps of the MIRROR Method – not through the improper exercise or abuse of authority during its implementation.

7. **Not without Question:** HR professionals or senior leaders who are tasked with supporting frontline leaders and managers through the MIRROR Method should not equate "support" with "blind and unconditional advocacy," particularly in the face of apparent concerns or explicit allegations of potentially dysfunctional behavior on the part of a specific leader. Allegations of leaders behaving or communicating in a dysfunctional manner need to be objectively assessed and addressed using the MIRROR Method.

8. **Overcoming Long-standing Dysfunction:** There is no question that holding individuals accountable is not easy, particularly when there have been long-standing issues with a person's behavior or performance that have not been addressed consistently, if at all, in the past. If individuals have been permitted

to behave improperly or perform at an unacceptable level for a prolonged period of time, they will be taken by surprise when told that this can no longer continue. Many employees in these circumstances become hostile and defensive when challenged. They often engage in personalized attacks against supervisors, become insubordinate in response to directives or requests for change and encourage day-to-day disrespect of leaders by others, by campaigning against them to coworkers.

The most effective and defensible way to address any type of inappropriate response to being investigated or performance managed is to objectively investigate and address the inappropriate response itself, using the MIRROR Method. That is, disrespect of a leader during a coaching discussion on some other matter needs to be investigated and remedied as a separate incident of dysfunction.

9. **The "Complex" Employee:** In situations involving "complex" employees (those with long-standing behavioral or performance issues or those faced with significant and complicated personal challenges), it is important for senior leaders and HR to work closely with and support leaders as they implement the MIRROR Method. Sometimes, this calls for the regular involvement of more than one supervisor or leader; at times it also requires the retaining of external consultants for support, including medical and legal experts as necessary.

10. **Role of Senior Leadership:** While senior leaders do not have to be directly involved in every step of the MIRROR Method, they should be involved in these two functions.

- Senior managers should be expected to objectively review and remedy insubordination of and disrespect towards frontline leaders in the course of their implementation of the MIRROR Method.

- Senior managers should be expected to inquire into and review (or oversee the review of) any concerns of dysfunctional conduct or communication regarding one of their direct reports.

In all other situations, senior leadership should play an oversight role, ensuring that the MIRROR Method is being implemented consistently, objectively and properly by those hired and qualified to do so (including operational leaders, HR personnel or external contractors).

11. **Who and When:** Not every leader on a team has to be involved in every step of the MIRROR Method. Frontline leaders (including unionized forepersons, supervisors and team leaders) often will be involved in "M – Monitoring;" frontline leaders, managers and human resources will be involved in "I – Inquiry and the Triage Process;" frontline leaders may conduct "R – informal Reviews" while managers, human resources or external contractors will perform formal Reviews; operational leaders, with input from human resources and others will determine and implement "R – the Remedial Plans;" external consultants likely will facilitate

"O – Operational Restoration;" and frontline leaders/ managers and human resources will be involved with the final "R – Revisiting the scene of the original dysfunction" to assess whether it has, in fact, been addressed successfully.

The organization is deemed to be aware of workplace dysfunction as soon as any leader, at any level of the organization, becomes aware of it. Accordingly, the roles and responsibilities of each leader and department should be clearly and explicitly established at a systemic level to avoid unnecessary delays and inaction caused by a lack of timely communication, miscommunication or any other type of dysfunction within or between leaders and departments in the course of implementing the MIRROR Method. Each supervisor and leader on the operational team should be made aware of and accountable for the procedural step(s) for which they are responsible. Similarly, each department should be clear on their respective jurisdiction and responsibilities in relation to the various steps in this process.

Step 1

MONITORING THE WORKPLACE

No team, regardless of its "success," is dysfunction-free. Dysfunction happens at every workplace, in every team, in different ways and at unpredictable times. The health of a team lies – not in avoiding or preventing dysfunction – but in addressing and resolving it as soon as it appears.

Dysfunction can only be addressed if it is detected; and detection of dysfunction can only happen if leaders are aware of workplace dynamics (and changes in those dynamics) on an ongoing basis.

This is why Monitoring is the first step of the MIRROR Method.

In this step, leaders are expected to proactively Monitor the:

- behavior/performance of individual team members;

- dynamics between team members on the same or different teams; and

- overall "climate," productivity and health of the team, in order to determine if there is potential dysfunction that needs to be resolved.

Once *potential* issues (or Dots of dysfunction) are detected, the other steps of the MIRROR Method are triggered.

The Value of Monitoring

Why is Monitoring of the workplace so important?

As noted previously, leaders are now expected to do more than simply respond or react to a formal complaint of workplace dysfunction. Leaders are expected to inquire into dysfunction of which they *are* or *should be* aware, as soon as they become alerted to it.

It is not only a professional/legal expectation to inquire into and resolve workplace dysfunction as soon as it becomes apparent, it is also far more practical and cost effective to engage in early resolution of these issues. The longer a dysfunctional situation is allowed to continue, the worse it becomes. As outlined previously, one tense or heated discussion, which results from or leads to misunderstandings between individuals, can result in significant costs to those individuals, their team and the overall organization if not dealt with immediately. As time passes, such dysfunction intensifies and builds rifts between individuals, draws others into the drama and distracts individuals from their core responsibilities at work.

Time *does not* heal wounds, particularly when it comes to workplace dysfunction. To the contrary, ignoring wounds causes them to fester, resulting in significant and unnecessary emotional and financial costs to the individuals involved and many others.

Accordingly, it is critical for leaders to Monitor the workplace for Dots of dysfunction, those definable, discreet dysfunctional incidents, interactions or dynamics.

What Are Dots?

Dots of dysfunction include any operational processes, leadership practices, individual conduct, communication or performance or interpersonal/team dynamics that in any way interfere with the ability of individuals and/or teams to function effectively and productively. It is irrelevant if a Dot is intentional or unintentional or culpable (within an individual's control) or non-culpable (partially or wholly outside an individual's control). All that matters is that the Dot in question is potentially interfering with the functioning of an individual or team.

In order to Monitor for Dots, a leader first needs to ask the following questions:

1. What are the core duties and expectations of the individuals on the team?

2. What is the core purpose and mandate of the overall team?

The leader then needs to ask:

3. Are the individuals on this team performing their respective duties at an acceptable level and in an acceptable manner? Are they meeting the core expectations of the organization?

4. Is the team delivering its services to the extent and in a manner expected by the organization?

More specifically, is something or someone interfering with what needs to be accomplished by an individual or the team? Is productivity low? Are delays/waitlists high? Are errors increasing? Are there issues with quality or delivery of service? Are there complaints, internal or external, about an individual's performance, behavior or communication?

Dots may include any of the following:

- dysfunctional behavior/performance/communication by specific individuals, including leaders;

- dysfunctional behavior between members of the same team or different teams;

- dysfunction between individuals and third parties, including clients, consumers and members of the public; and/or

- dysfunction among the team as a whole. In larger organizations, it also may include dysfunction between particular teams/departments.

As previously outlined (see Chapter 2, Workplace Dysfunction and the Changing Legal Landscape), if Dots of dysfunction are not addressed in an early and effective manner, they will transform into a costly train wreck. Train wrecks may take different forms, such as team breakdowns, permanent disability leaves, significant litigation and intense unmanageable turnover and staffing issues. Regardless of how they manifest themselves, all train wrecks result in a loss of trust and healthy communication between individuals or among a team in general. All cause significant damage to the personal and professional lives of those involved. And all take significant time to remedy.

Respectful workplaces focus on avoiding and preventing train wrecks – and their resulting emotional, psychological and organizational carnage – by actively Monitoring individual and team dynamics on a regular basis, in order to detect Dots of dysfunction and deal with them as soon as they appear.

Figure 10
DEALING WITH IT AT THE DOT

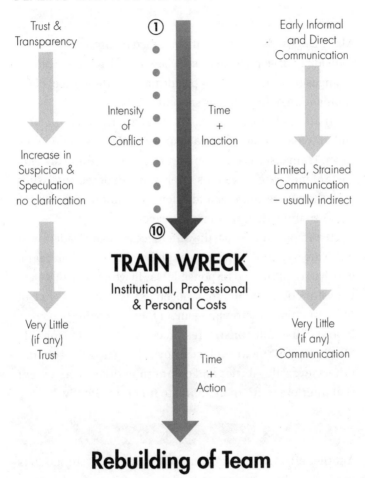

Trust &
Transparency

①

Early Informal
and Direct
Communication

Intensity
of
Conflict

Time
+
Inaction

Increase in
Suspicion &
Speculation
no clarification

Limited, Strained
Communication
– usually indirect

⑩

TRAIN WRECK
Institutional, Professional
& Personal Costs

Very Little
(if any)
Trust

Time
+
Action

Very Little
(if any)
Communication

Rebuilding of Team

How to Monitor for Dots

Many Dots of dysfunction are detected by simply observing individuals at work. In doing so, leaders can detect and address changes in an individual's performance, attendance, communication or behavior as soon they arise.

It also is helpful for leaders to regularly observe how individuals interact with each other, and those outside the team. Team discussions, e-mail correspondence and internal instant messenger systems often assist in detecting issues with the nature, manner and extent of communication by or between individuals at the workplace.

It is important to note the difference between leaders who cultivate day-to-day awareness of dynamics on their team, which is a healthy and responsible way in which to detect Dots of dysfunction, and micromanagement, which often is a Dot of dysfunction. Micromanagement is not a specific behavior, in and of itself. It constitutes excessive and unreasonable Monitoring of the workplace by over-inserting oneself into others' everyday duties and communications, to an extent that interferes with their ability to function effectively.

TALK TO THE TEAM

Another effective way to Monitor for Dots of dysfunction is to regularly interact and communicate with staff, informally throughout the day/week and more formally, through structured one-on-one meetings. These meetings can take place by having regularly scheduled check-ins, annual performance reviews or workplace surveys (preferably performed in person rather than in writing).

Mandatory exit interviews, when conducted properly and

objectively by an individual at arm's length from the specific team yet well versed in operations, can be a valuable resource for detecting Dots, some of which may have contributed to the departure of the individual being interviewed.

Direct communication with staff can be rich and enlightening but only if it takes place at the early stages of dysfunction, when the Dots are relatively minor and infrequent and there is fundamental trust and communication between leaders and their teams.

During these discussions, staff will commonly disclose concerns about potential dysfunction that they have observed or are experiencing with colleagues, clients and others. They often do so to seek guidance on what they can or should do about the situation (i.e., coaching for resolution) or to secure active and direct intervention and support from the leader.

FACILITATE AND MONITOR DEPARTMENT/TEAM COMMUNICATION AND MEETINGS

Regular team meetings are another way to detect potential Dots.

Leaders should Monitor meetings and overall team communication for the following potential Dots of dysfunction:

- conscious seat selection and location (distance from particular individuals, cliquey behavior among certain subsets of the team);

- exclusive huddling;

- side-chats and whispering;

- private note-writing and exchanges;

- disengagement and actively shutting down;

- dismissive or contemptuous facial expressions, dramatic sighing and other non-verbal behavior;

- sarcastic laughter not genuinely exhibited in jest;
- interrupting of others;
- talking over others;
- openly engaging in personalized attacks or sarcastic/derisive commentary; and
- prematurely exiting or ending the meeting in a dramatic manner to "send" a message to others.

These behaviors are not only Dots that need to be addressed; they often reflect the existence of other dysfunction occurring in the workplace.

When Dots come to the attention of the leader, the MIRROR Method is triggered. (If the MIRROR Method isn't triggered after the leader has learned about a Dot, the leader becomes at least partially responsible for any ongoing, subsequent dysfunction.)

Institutional Metrics

The Dots that have been outlined so far often become apparent through observations of and communications with staff. An alternative way to detect potential dysfunction is to examine metrics associated with the team. Metrics may include a review of available statistics on:

- productivity/output;
- error rates;
- sales/service;
- individual/team attendance/sick leave; and
- team turnover.

If leaders see unacceptably low metrics or a sudden deterioration in a particular metric, they should consider conducting an environmental scan to better understand the metrics and become aware of potential Dots that might explain the statistics.

Environmental Scans

If a leader is aware of issues or changes among individuals or the team yet cannot discern potential Dots, the leader may choose to initiate an environmental scan. A scan is usually conducted by a third party (unrelated to the team or organization) who specializes in team dynamics and dysfunction. This person engages in highly confidential interviews with each team member, including the leaders. It is a mandatory and all-inclusive process.

During the interviews, team members are given a safe and unstructured opportunity to share with the neutral third party what, from their perspective, is working on the team and what is not. Details and examples of dysfunction are provided to the third party in strict confidence. That information is then relayed to senior leadership (not the direct leaders) in a manner that protects the identity of those who provided the information.

Through this process, senior leaders are provided with collective input from team members about potential Dots of dysfunction without putting specific individuals in a vulnerable, unsafe or awkward position.

Scans often reveal concerns with the behavior or performance of certain individuals, dysfunctional leadership practices, inconsistent application of operational policies or dysfunctional dynamics among staff or between staff and frontline leaders. Usually, a number of different Dots are identified some of which may relate to each other and some of which are stand-alone concerns.

It is important to note that the results of the scans trigger the next step of the MIRROR Method, the Duty to Inquire (including the Triage Process), to determine next steps. All too often, leaders react to the results of the scan in the same way as a formal investigation. Scans are not formal investigations. There is no respondent being investigated and there is no due process in relation to any particular individual. Therefore, none of the Dots should be considered or handled as findings against anyone. Instead, the information should be treated in the same way as information obtained through any other process of detecting Dots, that is, by following through with the remaining steps of the MIRROR Method.

MYTH: If an employee is constantly making complaints about others, the leader can stop looking into their concerns.

REALITY: A leader can never stop inquiring into potential dysfunction, regardless of who brings the concern forward. However, if a leader properly applies the MIRROR Method to concerns and finds that an employee continues to bring forward unfounded alarms about others, that person's behavior becomes a Dot that needs to be managed.

Dots by Leaders

A common challenge is when Dots of dysfunction relate to the conduct, communication or performance of a leader. As set out in previous chapters, there are many leadership practices that are dysfunctional and interfere with the ability of the team to function effectively and productively.

When these Dots of dysfunction arise, it is often difficult and unrealistic to expect employees to bring them to the attention of the leader directly. In these circumstances, the organization should establish and communicate to employees ways in which they may relay their Dots to more senior leaders on the team, human resources or otherwise. Individuals who then receive reports of Dots from employees should implement the MIRROR Method to objectively review and address them as necessary.

Dots on Other Teams

Often, leaders observe or learn about potentially inappropriate behavior or poor performance of an individual who reports to someone else. Commonly, that person's behavior, communication or performance is creating dysfunction on their team but the individual is not a member of the team. What happens then?

The leader cannot ignore the issue, not only because it may be interfering with individuals on his/her team but also because once any leader knows of any workplace dysfunction, the organization as a whole is deemed to be aware of that dysfunction, regardless of who reports to whom.

MYTH: A leader can ignore dysfunction by those outside his/her team.

REALITY: As soon as a leader (in any capacity) becomes aware of potential dysfunction, then the organization is deemed to be aware of that same dysfunction. Leaders cannot ignore reports or observations of dysfunction by those on a different team. Leaders should approach their own leader, the leader of the other team or human resources to report their awareness of potential dysfunction and then allow others to deal with it through the MIRROR Method.

While the leader needs to act, he/she should not take over the situation or address the employee directly, given that the individual reports to a different leader. It is important to respect the overall organizational structure and associated reporting protocols, when it comes to the MIRROR Method and otherwise.

To align the duty to Monitor for Dots with the duty to respect the organizational structure, the leader should report the potential dysfunction to that person's leader (either directly or through his/her own leader). The individual's leader (or broader leadership team) will then be responsible for implementing the MIRROR Method.

Dots by Other Leaders

Sometimes, a leader observes inappropriate, unethical or dysfunctional behavior by a leader on a different team (or in a different leadership position on their team). This, too, is a Dot that needs to be reviewed. It triggers the leader's obligations to act, both as leader and as bystander (and sometimes, as a complainant/recipient of the behavior).

In this situation, the leader should report the concerns to senior leadership or human resources. Those individuals will then be responsible for ensuring the Dot is assessed and addressed through the MIRROR Method.

Don'ts Related to Dots

While leaders should actively engage and communicate with their teams to Monitor for signs and symptoms of dysfunction, it is important that, in doing so, they make the situation better for their team, not worse.

Some don'ts of Monitoring Dots, which could inadvertently contribute to the dysfunctional environment, include:

- *Asking* staff to monitor other staff for performance/ attendance/behavioral issues (unless they are a designated mentor and the monitoring is done in a transparent manner as part of a learning plan or otherwise);

- *Asking* staff general questions about the performance of other specific staff unless these questions take place as part of a formal performance review or investigation of which the person is aware;

- *Sharing* with certain staff concerns or frustrations regarding a particular staff member's performance/ behavior;

- *Informing* staff that a particular staff member is being performance managed, disciplined or monitored; and

- *Asking* staff to confirm/corroborate the leader's suspicions or specific concerns about a particular staff member. Any Dots from staff should come from them, unprompted and at their own initiative or through open-ended questions posed during a review/ investigation.

It is important for leaders to be *receptive* and *responsive* to staff concerns regarding other staff/leaders. However, outside the necessary inquiries that flow from and relate to a formal, confidential investigation, leaders should respect the dignity and privacy of staff by refraining from discussing concerns about performance/behavior with others on the team. This practice, intentional or not, is disrespectful to the individual involved and divisive and destructive to the team as a whole.

Now What? Dealing with It at the Dot

"Dealing with it at the Dot" does not mean that leaders should blindly accept concerns reported by one employee about another, prematurely judge the actions or intentions of individual staff members or quickly shut down situations, based solely on the detection of Dots during the Monitoring process.

The detection of Dots requires leaders to initiate the MIRROR Method as soon as possible. This will result in a timely and objective evaluation of the situation, an accurate understanding and diagnosis of the dysfunction and the implementation of a timely remedy to resolve the problem.

MYTH: Leaders can "give it some time" to see if the dysfunction resolves itself.

REALITY: Leaders need to inquire into potential dysfunction as soon they become aware of it. Time and inaction will not resolve dysfunction; it will only make it worse.

Step 2

INQUIRING INTO THE DOT

Once a potential Dot has been observed or reported, leaders must assess the potential severity of the Dot in order to determine the next steps.

The "I" of the MIRROR Method helps leaders assess this severity by Inquiring into Dots of dysfunction as soon they arise. This step helps leaders determine whether they should review a Dot informally or formally based on the nature and extent of concerns that have come forward.

Too many organizations ignore this phase and engage in a one-size-fits-all approach to their review of workplace dysfunction.

In some workplaces, the nature of review conducted is dictated by those individuals who have come forward to report their concerns. Some demand that the organization take formal steps immediately to deal with the situation regardless of how "minor" the Dot might be. Others demand that the organization do absolutely nothing with the reported concern, regardless of how serious the Dot might be. These organizations take their lead on next steps from these employees, regardless of the potential costs and risks that flow from this decision.

MYTH: Leaders do not have to act on reported concerns if the staff member asks them not to.

REALITY: Leaders need to monitor and inquire into all issues that are brought to their attention. The extent of their intervention will be based on the results of the Triage Process, not on the desires or demands of the employees who have come forward.

In other organizations, next steps are dictated by specific leaders based on their leadership styles or personal opinions of those involved. At one end of the spectrum, there are leaders who informally review situations and coach individuals regardless of the potential seriousness associated with the Dot behavior. These leaders repeatedly have "off-the-record" discussions with staff regarding their performance/behavioral concerns, regardless of how ineffective such coaching has been, and then wonder why the problem continues to resurface. They rarely, if ever, escalate a situation to a formal review that results in formal discipline or formal performance management of the individual involved.

At the other end of the spectrum are leaders who formally review and investigate all Dots regardless of how potentially insignificant or uncommon they might be, either in relation to a particular individual (having a bad day) or regarding team dynamics in general. These leaders have very few informal meetings or coaching discussions with staff; instead, they investigate every matter in a structured, rigid manner, with the air of formal accountability and potential punishment surrounding it.

In certain circumstances, leaders will determine next steps based on the identity of the individual who reports the concern or the identity of the person being reported. Their personal opinions of the individuals involved influence their decision as to whether or how to review a Dot of dysfunction. As set out previously, this is wholly unacceptable and itself constitutes a Dot of dysfunction that needs to be reviewed and addressed by the organization.

Next steps and, more specifically, the type of review to conduct after detecting a Dot of dysfunction should not be dictated by the wishes of the employees who come forward or the preferences or personal opinions of the leaders involved. Instead, this should be determined by carefully considering the information that has come forward and then determining where, on the Scale of Dysfunctional Conduct, it *might* fall.

This is called the "Triage Process."

Summary of the Triage Process

There are three steps to the Triage Process.

1. Obtain further, more specific details about the observed or reported Dots and deconstruct any broad generalizations or characterizations ("labels") associated with the reported concerns into specific behaviors or practices.

2. Determine the nature of review to conduct (informal or formal) based on the potential seriousness of the Dots and set up any necessary containment measures associated with the need for a formal review (for example, determining if particular individuals need to be placed on administrative leave or whether certain individuals, including leaders, need to be moved or separated pending the review).

Figure 11
THE TRIAGE PROCESS

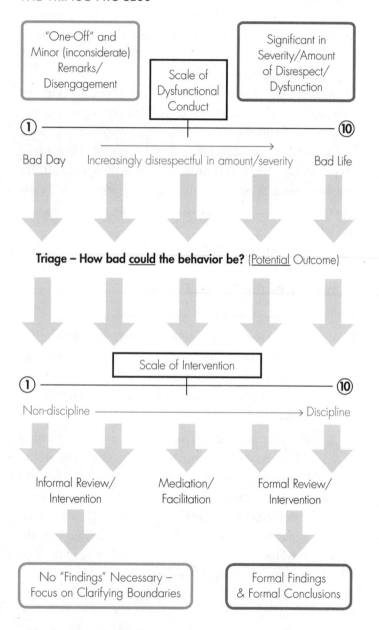

"One-Off" and Minor (inconsiderate) Remarks/ Disengagement

Scale of Dysfunctional Conduct

Significant in Severity/Amount of Disrespect/ Dysfunction

① ──────────────── ⑩

Bad Day   Increasingly disrespectful in amount/severity   Bad Life

Triage – How bad <u>could</u> the behavior be? (<u>Potential</u> Outcome)

Scale of Intervention

① ──────────────── ⑩

Non-discipline ──────────────→ Discipline

Informal Review/ Intervention

Mediation/ Facilitation

Formal Review/ Intervention

No "Findings" Necessary – Focus on Clarifying Boundaries

Formal Findings & Formal Conclusions

3. Advise those who have come forward (in a general way that does not breach others' confidentiality) of the results of the Triage Process and more specifically how the leader plans to objectively review the reported Dots. As part of this, the leader should advise those involved of the clear expectations of confidentiality and non-retaliation related to the concerns they have reported and any resulting review.

Examining Each Step in Detail

1. GATHERING INFORMATION/ DECONSTRUCTING LABELS

In many situations, individuals report Dots using general characterizations of others' performance, behavior or communication. Terms used to describe concerns often include "unproductive," "incompetent," "disengaged," "bullying," "aggressive" and so on. None of these terms describe behaviors that can be properly Triaged. They are simply labels.

Leaders need to deconstruct these labels to better understand the specific behaviors and performance issues that form the Dot.

Labels are deconstructed by asking the following:

■ What is meant by the term "incompetent/disengaged/ bullying" (and so on)?

■ In the dynamic or situation with which they are faced, what specific interaction, communication, task, practice or behavior forms the basis upon which the term "incompetent/disengaged/bullying" (and so on) has been used?

In addition, when complaining about others, individuals often describe their own reactions and emotions in response to the Dot. They report feeling "anxious," "intimidated," "silenced," "stressed" and so on. Just as labels of others' behavior should not be Triaged, neither should emotional reactions to those behaviors.

Instead, those emotions should be deconstructed as follows:

- What specific interaction, communication or behavior involving the other person has caused this person to feel anxious or intimidated?

- In what specific way did this individual find that behavior or communication intimidating or stressful?

After leaders gather this information and deconstruct the labels, they should end the meeting with the person who has come forward with the concerns. Leaders should refrain from committing to or communicating with this individual about next steps, even if pressured to do so.

MYTH: Leaders should not act on reported dysfunction unless they have witnessed or experienced the disrespect themselves.

REALITY: Leaders are expected to inquire and intervene into potential dysfunction whether or not they have observed or experienced it directly. Commonly, individuals will not engage in dysfunctional conduct when a leader is present and often behave very differently towards leaders than lateral colleagues or staff reporting to them (a practice commonly referenced as "managing up").

---

2. DETERMINING THE TYPE OF REVIEW

After observing or receiving information concerning specific Dots (either through staff members, metrics or scans), leaders should Triage the Dots based on the potential severity of the concerns in question.

In doing so, the leaders should ask, if the alleged Dots are found to be true (through an objective review): How serious could they be? Where would they fall on the Scale of Dysfunctional Conduct?

To assist in making this determination, leaders should ask a number of questions, including those listed here.

If the allegations are true, might they:

- result in formal discipline, including dismissal, of the individual(s) involved?

- result in adverse media coverage for the individual(s) and/or the organization?

- result in safety, labor, civil or criminal litigation for individual(s) and/or the organization?

- attract the attention of regulatory agencies overseeing the individual(s) or organization?

- adversely affect the overall reputation of the organization, if brought to the attention of the public?

If the answer to any of the foregoing is "yes," then the organization should conduct a formal review. If the answer is "no," then the leader may review and resolve the matter using an informal approach.

If a formal review is required, the leaders involved in this process also should consider whether the potential risks related to the Dot need to be contained or mitigated by placing particular individuals on leave from work or by separating certain individuals at the workplace, pending the outcome of the review.

3. COMMUNICATING WITH INDIVIDUALS INVOLVED

After leaders have determined next steps, they should circle back to those who have come forward, those who are the subject of concern as well as others who may be involved (witnesses, bystanders and other leaders) to confidentially and clearly outline their overall plan for reviewing and addressing Dots that have been identified. That is, individuals need to be told if they will be involved in a mandated mediation, team-building session or formal investigation.

By having this transparent follow-up discussion with the individuals about next steps, the leader is seen to be taking action in response to concerns not by blindly accepting those concerns but by objectively reviewing them. This will encourage other individuals to come forward in the future. In the absence of having a discussion of this nature, many individuals assume, often mistakenly, that leaders have ignored their concerns. As a result, they refrain from reporting further issues that subsequently arise in the workplace.

Other Aspects of the Triage Process

The results of the Triage Process will help leaders address other procedural issues that commonly arise when Dots are reported or identified.

ANONYMITY

Many leaders wonder if they should/can keep the names of complainants anonymous.

If, following the Triage Process, the leaders determine that a formal review is necessary, it is not possible, defensible or respectful of the respondent to maintain anonymity surrounding the concerns that have come forward. Those accused of allegations in a formal review/investigation are entitled to full disclosure of the particulars of the Dots, including the names of the complainants and witnesses and the circumstances involved.

If, however, an informal review/approach seems most appropriate, it may well be possible to keep the names of complainants confidential (particularly if the informal intervention simply involves communicating and clarifying workplace expectations, without involving any evaluation of or formal criticism surrounding particular events).

Again, it is not up to the particular employees or leaders involved to determine whether concerns should remain anonymous; it is dictated exclusively by the results of the Triage Process.

REPRESENTATION AT INTERVIEWS

In informal reviews, there is no legal requirement to have union or other types of representation available for the discussion. Many times they participate, as an observer or to support the individual participating in the interview, but this is not a legal requirement.

During formal reviews, representation should be present for all interviews, particularly that of the respondent. Failure to have a union or other legal representative present for an investigation will usually void any formal discipline rendered as a result of the review.

In a similar vein, non-unionized employees, including leaders, should be invited to bring a support person to formal reviews/investigations into their conduct or performance.

Leaders often wonder whether they can direct staff to "deal with issues" themselves. This, too, can only be determined through the Triage Process.

If the matter is sufficiently serious to warrant formal intervention, then leaders must become involved and deal with the Dot directly. If the matter is relatively minor and falls at the mild end of the Scale of Dysfunctional Conduct, then the leader can encourage staff to deal with issues themselves directly, rather than handing it off to the leader to resolve.

MYTH: Leaders can direct employees to deal with the dysfunction themselves.

REALITY: Leaders need to actively support their employees in resolving workplace dysfunction.

For minor issues, they can encourage employees to address matters themselves and can coach employees on how to do so. If an employee does not feel comfortable having the MIRROR conversation, the leader should facilitate that discussion.

For potentially serious dysfunction, leaders must intervene directly to address the situation, using the MIRROR Method, and cannot delegate this task to staff.

The leaders may still be involved, by coaching and supporting staff in relation to their direct discussions with each other or by facilitating these discussions themselves but the leaders do not have to "take over" simply because staff expect them to do so.

Summary

The type of review to conduct following the detection of a Dot depends entirely on the results of the Triage Process; it should not be influenced by the preferences or comfort levels of leaders or the demands made by particular staff or individuals who have come forward.

Once the Triage Process is complete, leaders then conduct an objective Review of the complaint, concerns or observations that have come forward, which is Step 3 in the MIRROR Method.

Step 3

CONDUCTING THE REVIEW

Regardless of whether the Review of the Dot is informal or formal, it is critical that every Review is conducted:

- shortly after the concerns come forward;

- in a confidential manner;

- in a manner that protects everyone involved from retaliation and/or improper influence;

- within a reasonable period of time after it begins, with no undue delay;

- in an objective manner, ensuring that all relevant evidence, perspectives and perceptions are considered, including those of the person "accused" of the concerning behavior/performance;

- in a genuinely respectful manner, with curious and open-minded questions; and

- in a neutral manner, by someone who is not biased or seen to be biased against or in favor of anyone involved.

No type of Review, informal or formal, justifies any leader blindly accepting or acting upon one person's "story," concern or perspective or automatically ignoring or dismissing the perspective of others. No leader should ever get "sucked into the drama of the first story" (or the last) however compelling or enticing it might be.

Informal Review/Intervention

As set out in the Triage Process, informal Reviews are conducted when allegations are not considered sufficiently serious to warrant discipline. Accordingly, Reviews of this nature are not conducted to make formal findings of fact. Instead, the purpose is to clarify expectations, improve communication, strengthen relationships and re-establish boundaries moving forward.

During informal Reviews, the assessment of past incidents or generally dysfunctional dynamics is conducted primarily to bring to an individual's attention perceived concerns regarding his/her behavior/performance and, if confirmed, explore how to remedy these concerns moving forward.

THE MIRROR DISCUSSION

Many individuals in the workplace, including those who come forward with concerns about others, are commonly unaware of how they are "showing up," impacting others and contributing to the overall dysfunction. Very few individuals approach their day with the intent to disrupt, interfere with or upset others. While they have a responsibility to change their behavior, they are not expected to be mind readers. They deserve to be provided with a clear picture of their Dot issues in a respectful manner, be given a fair opportunity to respond and be allowed a genuine opportunity to change.

Accordingly, in informal Reviews, the leader should facilitate one or more MIRROR conversations with *everyone* involved, using descriptive and non-inflammatory terminology to describe how they are "seen" by others generally or how specific issues with their behaviors or performance are being perceived/experienced by others.

Each person should be given a fair chance to respond to this mirrored feedback. The response may be an outright denial that the behavior occurred at all; it might involve agreement that the behavior occurred but accompanied with an explanation surrounding that behavior, including important history about the individuals involved, the incident in question and/or the contributing role of others; or it might involve an explanation about personal or professional factors that influenced the particular behavior or conduct in question.

The person's response to the feedback needs to be received and considered in a compassionate manner with an open mind. There is no justification for a leader dismissing or becoming defensive to information of this nature. Doing so suggests potential pre-judgment on the part of the leader.

The leader needs to evaluate the initial Dot concerns in light of this information before taking next steps. If the Dot concerns were reported to the leader, the leader needs to have a similar MIRROR conversation with the other individual(s) (and the leader may need to implement informal remedies in relation to that individual as well).

The MIRROR discussion is a critical step in any Review, informal or formal, as many individuals are not aware of the concerns surrounding their behavior/performance or the impact they are allegedly having on others.

There are different ways in which to conduct these MIRROR conversations during an *informal* Review.

- If the Dot concerns appear to involve only one individual, then the leader should meet with that individual alone, to provide the MIRROR feedback, hear his/her perspective on the feedback, determine whether or not the Dot behavior is confirmed and, if so, design a remedy (the next step of the MIRROR Method).

- If the Dot of dysfunction appears to be *interpersonal* rather than *unilateral*, the leader can facilitate an informal discussion in which each person involved in the dysfunction participates directly in a MIRROR discussion with the other. Following this, they should work out a practical plan, with the leader's assistance and input, to repair their working relationship moving forward. This is not imposed by the leader, but is created by the parties and can take place without the leader having to make any determination or impose any remedy, informal or otherwise.

- If there is more than one person involved in the dynamic and a facilitated discussion has either been attempted – unsuccessfully – or does not seem practical in the circumstances, the leader should have a MIRROR conversation with each person separately, hear their perspectives, determine what transpired (on a balance of probabilities) and then design informal individualized remedies in response.

Informal Reviews require leaders to inquire into concerns objectively, in an open-minded manner, using a compassionate and curious versus critical approach. Commonly, issues that first show up at the workplace, particularly those that fall at the mild end of the scale, reflect inter-personal dysfunction/misunderstandings that demand early resolution *between* individuals versus formalized expectations towards one of those involved. Leaders who get sucked into the drama of the first story, during informal Reviews, sometimes overlook this dynamic and end up informally resolving the wrong problem or only part of a problem.

MYTH: When leaders investigate concerns, they can keep the complainant's name confidential/anonymous.

REALITY: The complainant's name may or may not need to be disclosed during informal Reviews, depending on the particular situation. However, the name of the person who has come forward with concerns always will need to be disclosed in formal Reviews.

Even where the informal Reviews reflect issues with one particular person, the ultimate remedy will consist of clarifying expectations and providing support to that person. The goal is to determine whether there are dysfunctional behaviors/performance concerns and, if so, set the person up for success, not failure. The *manner* in which the informal Review is conducted plays a significant role in this process.

Formal Reviews

Proper formal investigations are the foundation to principled, evidence-based and defensible decision-making in the workplace.

Formal Reviews, when conducted objectively, will result in formal findings of fact regarding:

- what is *most likely* to have happened in the workplace on a given day or over a period of time; and

- who is *most likely* responsible for which of the dynamics involved.

Figure 12

THE BUILDING BLOCKS OF A FAIR REVIEW

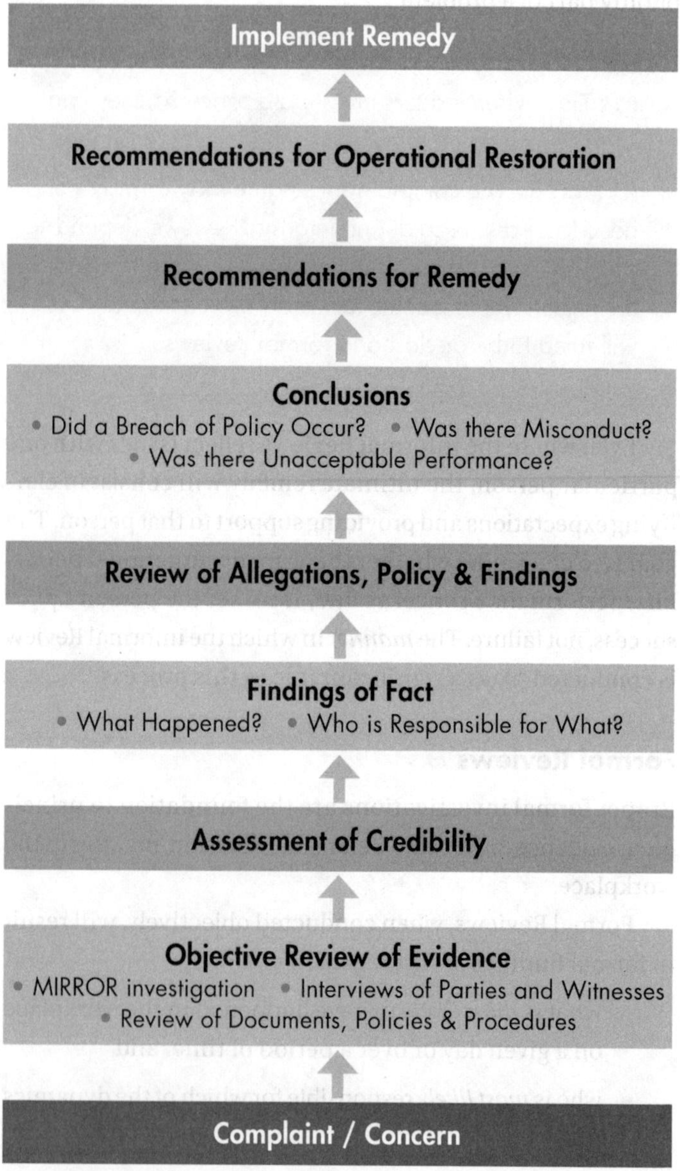

Implement Remedy

⬆

Recommendations for Operational Restoration

⬆

Recommendations for Remedy

⬆

Conclusions
- Did a Breach of Policy Occur?   • Was there Misconduct?
- Was there Unacceptable Performance?

⬆

Review of Allegations, Policy & Findings

⬆

Findings of Fact
- What Happened?   • Who is Responsible for What?

⬆

Assessment of Credibility

⬆

Objective Review of Evidence
- MIRROR investigation   • Interviews of Parties and Witnesses
- Review of Documents, Policies & Procedures

⬆

Complaint / Concern

These findings then form the basis of formal conclusions as to whether specific individuals have breached various particular workplace policies, procedures, professional codes of conduct, legislation or otherwise.

These conclusions then trigger the imposition of specific remedies that may include significant discipline, loss of employment, monetary fines and damages and general public scrutiny.

Given the potential severity of these consequences, it is imperative that organizations conduct a thorough and fair investigation. Their failure to do so will result in arriving at findings of fiction, not fact, leading to devastating outcomes for those involved.

THE SCOPE OF THE INVESTIGATION: PEELING THE ONION

Commonly, workplace dysfunction continues to repeat itself even after numerous investigations have been conducted. The same issues, or the same individuals, keep showing up as Dots.

This situation often happens because Reviews concerning generalized workplace dysfunction are being conducted in the same way as Reviews of discreet incidents of workplace misconduct.

In cases of misconduct, such as theft, the focus is on determining who did it. However, with workplace dysfunction, the concern is often not based on one particular incident or caused by one specific person. Rather, it frequently includes various dynamics between different individuals, all of whom own their piece of the "poisoned pie."

In order to ensure the complexities surrounding workplace dysfunction are properly and accurately reviewed, rather than asking "who did it," it is more appropriate to ask:

- what is most likely happening here; and
- who is most likely responsible for what part of this dynamic.

AN EXAMPLE

Cathy is a nurse who works on a medical unit at a hospital. It is a high paced, demanding job that requires the right combination of accuracy and timeliness.

For the past few months, Cathy has been making medication errors, not answering patient call bells, leaving early and coming in late. As a result, Cathy has created more work for and pressure on the other nurses.

Cathy's coworkers have gone to Beth, the nurse manager, for assistance.

Beth approached Cathy with the team's concerns. Cathy downplayed the situation and told Beth that she has a number of confidential, personal issues going on and needs support not criticism. Cathy said she felt "harassed" by Beth coming to her with this concern.

Beth advised the team that she had spoken to Cathy but said nothing further.

Over time, the rest of the team became increasingly bitter and resentful, not to mention exhausted. They stopped having much to do with Cathy because they grew tired of it being "all about her."

Cathy approached Beth to complain that others were leaving her out, going on breaks together, huddling and whispering together at the desk and responding to her in a curt manner. Cathy provided Beth with a number of examples and asked her to investigate.

A narrow, traditional scope of this Review might be framed as follows: has the team been inappropriate in leaving Cathy out or does Cathy's specific complaint have merit?

This narrow scope would result in only one of two alternative outcomes.

First, the complaint against Cathy's coworkers might be allowed and the team would be held accountable for their conduct. Because it was a Review into Cathy's complaint, nothing would be done about the fact that she triggered some of the others' behaviors and has contributed to the dysfunctional environment.

Alternatively, Cathy's complaint would be dismissed, and the team would (wrongly) think they hadn't done anything wrong since, in their view, it was all caused by her initial behavior/performance.

Either of these outcomes would create resentment and frustration on the part of those who were held accountable for their particular contributions when others were not. The problem would not be resolved, only aggravated, and the dysfunction would continue.

A more appropriate and effective way to Review this matter is to ask what is most likely happening between Cathy and her coworkers and who is responsible for what part of this situation.

In approaching the dynamics in this broad manner, as a layered onion that needs to be peeled, a number of *potential* issues may need to be reviewed and evaluated:

- Cathy's performance and productivity issues;

- Cathy's failure to acknowledge or take responsibility for these issues;

- the coworkers' disrespectful conduct towards Cathy;

- Beth's failure to properly address the team's concerns about Cathy in a timely manner or hold Cathy to an acceptable standard at work; and

- any other issues that might arise during the course of the Review itself.

HOW SHOULD THE FORMAL REVIEW BE CONDUCTED? A SUMMARY OF A DEFENSIBLE INVESTIGATION

Regardless of scope, all formal Reviews need to be conducted in an objective and respectful manner, with strict adherence to the procedural rights of those involved in the investigation. These include, at minimum:

- strict confidentiality on the part of everyone being interviewed or investigated (parties and witnesses);

- no indirect or direct retaliation of or improper influence by *anyone* towards those being interviewed or investigated;

- right of the respondent to know the allegations being made against him/her, including the specific particulars surrounding the incidents/dynamics being investigated; and

- right of the respondent (and, commonly, anyone else involved) to have a representative or support person accompany them to the interview.

Formal Reviews should be conducted by excluded (non-unionized) managers, human resource professionals or external consultants. Anyone who conducts a formal Review should be trained and experienced in conducting fair and objective workplace investigations.

Finally, the investigator should be neutral and perceived as neutral by everyone involved in the investigation. If there is any possibility of an investigator being biased or seen as biased in favor of or against a particular party, that investigator should recuse him/herself and allow someone else to conduct the investigation.

MYTH: Leaders should not act if there are no witnesses and it is a "he said/she said" situation.

REALITY: Leaders are expected to inquire, intervene into and remedy dysfunction whether or not there are any witnesses. Leaders cannot be "on the fence" when it comes to workplace dysfunction. Decisive, clear and respectful decision-making is the foundation of strong leadership.

Generally speaking, investigators should interview all relevant witnesses and evaluate documents (including workplace-related documents, e-mails, texts and relevant Facebook posts and other social media material) prior to interviewing the respondent. (It is important to note that in many instances of workplace dysfunction there are no witnesses; the fact that the dysfunction is "he said/she said" is not a reason to ignore the matter.)

THE FIVE WS AND THE ONE H

When formally Reviewing workplace dysfunction, the five Ws in relation to each person's *perspective* are critical.

- What happened (in detail, deconstructing the labels)?

- Who was involved (including witnesses prior to, during and subsequent to any dysfunctional event or exchange)?

- Where did this take place (in detail)?

- When did this take place?

- Why did they respond (or not respond) to the exchange or event in the manner they did?

However, the one H is as important as the five Ws – the *how*. How did they – and others – act, speak or interact with each other? This discussion includes verbal and non-verbal behavior, facial expressions, as well as specific tone, delivery and overall demeanor associated with any communication.

INTERVIEW WITH THE RESPONDENT

After the initial portion of the Review is complete, the investigator should meet with the respondent to hear his/her perspective. This involves more than simply informing the respondent of the allegations against him/her and asking for confirmation or denial of the allegations. It involves allowing the respondent a fulsome opportunity to share his/her perspective on the allegations and overall workplace dynamics in question by answering the five Ws and the one H set out above.

The respondent also is entitled to provide any defense or explanation he/she might have, any alibi that might exist or any background or overall context that might be relevant.

The investigator should be sure to "put to" the respondent any evidence of others that is inconsistent with his/her version and allow him/her to respond.

By the conclusion of the interview, the respondent should be aware of the full extent of concerns in relation to his/her behavior or performance and should have been given a full, exhaustive opportunity to respond.

After hearing from the respondent, the investigator may need to interview additional relevant witnesses, review additional documents and/or re-interview prior witnesses, in order to give them an opportunity to hear and respond to what the respondent had to say.

> **MYTH:** During informal Reviews and discussions, an employee has no right to defend him/herself. The "right to be heard" only arises in formal investigations.
>
> **REALITY:** An objective and proper Review of workplace dysfunction and dynamics, whether informal or formal, ensures that all perspectives are considered, including and especially those of the person being "accused" of the inappropriate conduct/performance.

At times, complainants and witnesses may become respondents, if allegations or Dots arise against them during the course of the investigation. When this happens, these individuals must be informed of the change in their status and then given all procedural protections associated with their updated status as respondents.

FINDINGS OF FACT

Once all of the evidence has been collected, the investigator needs to determine, on a balance of probabilities, what most likely happened and who is responsible for what parts of it.

A *balance of probabilities* requires the investigator to ask what is more likely than not to have happened between or among those involved in the workplace dynamics, after:

- considering the perspectives and experiences of everyone involved;

- examining the relevant documents and correspondence; and

- assessing the credibility of those involved (where versions as to what happened conflict).

In assessing "what most likely happened," the investigator is making objective "findings" of fact. These then form the basis for the investigator's conclusions.

CONCLUSIONS

After making objective findings of fact, the investigator must conclude whether the respondents' behavior, communication, conduct or performance is objectively viewed as unacceptable or inappropriate in the workplace.

Throughout the course of the Review, the investigator will have received numerous opinions as to whether the respondents' conduct was inappropriate, offensive or unacceptable. However, as discussed previously, conclusions regarding an individual's behavior or conduct should not be based on the opinions of anyone involved. Instead, the investigator must apply an objective standard of reasonableness to his/her findings of fact by asking, "Would a reasonable person, working in this jurisdiction, at this particular time, find this specific behavior/communication to be offensive, intimidating, discriminatory or otherwise?"

The answer to this question constitutes the objective "conclusions" of the investigator.

Investigators often seek legal, human resources or other expert advice and support prior to making conclusions as to whether their findings reflect or constitute a breach of particular legislation, safety regulations, codes of conduct and/or other workplace policies and operating procedures.

WRITTEN REPORT

Investigators should include their findings and conclusions in a written report. This report – or a summary of it – should be provided to those leaders involved with the management and oversight of the respondent in order to determine how to respond.

The development and implementation of this "response" forms part of the next step of the MIRROR Method – that of remedy.

Step 4

DESIGNING AND IMPLEMENTING INDIVIDUAL REMEDIES

I n Step 4 of the MIRROR Method, leaders design and implement a Remedy based on the objective results of the informal or formal reviews conducted into Dots of dysfunction.

Informal Remedies

An informal review of a situation results in an informal and non-disciplinary Remedy.

If the informal review concludes that the behavioral/ performance concerns fall at 1 or 2 on the Scale of Dysfunctional Conduct (see Figure 4 in Chapter 3), the leader should have a MIRROR discussion with the individual involved. If the conduct falls at 3 or 4 (or if this is the second or third discussion regarding the behavior at 1-2), then the MIRROR discussion should be followed up with a MIRROR letter, which clearly outlines the concerns and expectations set out during the MIRROR discussion.

The MIRROR discussion, referenced previously in Step 3, can also be used as a method of coaching individuals regarding workplace concerns and expectations as part of the informal Remedy. The purpose of the MIRROR discussion, at this stage, is to allow the leader to set out his/her conclusions (following the informal review) regarding concerns about the individual's performance/behavior *and* provide the individual with clear expectations moving forward.

This MIRROR discussion consists of the components described below.

- Set out for the individual, in a respectful manner with a measured tone, a clear reflection/picture of how he/she is behaving or performing at the workplace, using descriptive and non-inflammatory terminology, with specific conclusions reached by the leader (i.e., not labels).

- In contrast to the informal review, a MIRROR discussion at the Remedy stage is not the time for extensive employee input, debate or discussion into "what happened." This is the opportunity for the leader to communicate his/her findings and conclusions.

- Set out clear, specific and descriptive ways in which the person's performance and/or behavior must change in order to meet the expectations of the leader and the overall organization. This part of the discussion also should provide the individual with suggested replacement behaviors (e.g., next time you are concerned about Sam's communication with a customer, do not criticize him in front of the customer – instead, politely interrupt the discussion (if urgent) and take him aside to speak with him confidentially). It is not enough to tell individuals what they are doing wrong and then direct them to stop; it is equally important and necessary to share with them acceptable ways in which they can have their needs and concerns heard and addressed.

- The employee being told of the leader's concerns and expectations does not need to agree with these positions (nor does the leader need to seek such consensus). The employee simply needs to follow the direction being given.

- Set out specific supports that will be provided by the leader/organization to facilitate the expected changes. These may include refresher or new/additional training, mentoring, job-shadowing, adjustment of duties, structured performance plans and otherwise. At this stage of the discussion, the leader can explore with the individual other ways in which to assist him/her in effecting the necessary changes.

- Advise the individual that the leader will be monitoring the dynamics in the workplace for signs of improvements or continuing issues *and* in the face of continuing issues, the leader will be required to intervene and take further action.

- Offer the individual access to the Employee and Family Assistance Program (EFAP) as an overall support through this process.

Formal Remedies

Following formal reviews/investigations, leaders should design and implement Remedies based on the specific findings and conclusions in the report.

An investigation may determine that more than one individual has contributed to the workplace incident or dysfunction in question (regardless of how the concern/complaint was framed initially). For example, the complainant may have contributed to the workplace dysfunction or may have breached confidentiality during the review; a bystander may have ignored dysfunction he/she had observed; and the accused may have engaged in some or all of the unacceptable behavior that formed the basis of the complaint.

A one-size-fits-all approach to Remedying this dysfunctional situation will not result in sustainable success for the team. Employees deserve and will respond best to a customized Remedial Plan based on their role in the situation and the ongoing circumstances with which they are faced.

MYTH: Equality among team members demands that each team member be treated in a similar manner.

REALITY: Equality means treating individuals the same if they are engaging in similar ways. Leaders do not have to treat individuals the same as others if their behavior/performance is different from others.

Each person, in the above situation, would need his/her own Remedial Plan based on the specific findings and conclusions that relate to his/her conduct. This does not mean that each person involved would be given the same level of discipline or require the same type of supports. It simply means that each would be addressed, on an individualized basis, in a manner that reflects his/her degree of culpability in relation to the dysfunctional dynamics in question and the unique supports that may be required moving forward.

Hammers or Hugs?

Some organizations base Remedial Plans on accountability alone. They institute narrow legalistic disciplinary policies such as "three strikes and you're out," without regard for why those strikes arose in the first place and what might have been done to avoid them from recurring in the future. These organizations often rush to termination of challenging employees, without providing them with a full and fair opportunity to change, and without recognizing that, in some situations, employees who are challenging in some respects are of incredible value in others. In these situations, the most cost-effective, practical and humane answer lies in Remedying the issue, not removing the individual.

In contrast, other organizations exclusively base Remedial Plans on facilitating change through the provision of supports. They avoid discipline/accountability and focus on training, coaching and mentoring. Without accountability and consequences, however, many individuals do not genuinely believe they need to change their behavior and therefore they don't, despite the many conversations they have had and the numerous courses and coaching sessions they have been given.

The bottom line is that neither hammers (accountability) nor hugs (supports), on their own, will be successful in effecting lasting positive change for individuals or organizations. For change to occur, individuals need to be held accountable for their unacceptable behavior and performance, need to be clearly told of expectations moving forward, need to be given a fair opportunity to make changes and need to be offered supports to facilitate the necessary change.

Revisiting the "Why Does Not Justify the How" and Its Relevance to Remedy

Earlier in this book, we discussed three key concepts related to workplace dysfunction.

1. It is all about the How, in that workplace dysfunction commonly comes down to how individuals behave toward, communicate with and treat each other.

2. The Why does not justify the How, meaning that individuals cannot *justify* their inappropriate behavior or unacceptable performance on their personalities, personal struggles or issues with those around them.

3. While not a justification, it remains important to genuinely *understand* the Why in order to thoroughly address all of the dynamics at play, in relation to both the individual involved and the overall team.

In designing individual Remedial Plans, leaders should ensure they address the How by holding individuals *accountable* for their unacceptable behavior, performance or communication, through non-disciplinary or disciplinary measures, *and* make reasonable efforts to mitigate or address the Whys that contributed to the behavior, by providing the individual with specific customized *supports* to facilitate positive changes to their behavior/performance moving forward.

AN EXAMPLE OF REMEDYING THE HOW AND WHY

In one example, a senior employee was going through a contentious divorce and child custody battle. The objective review *confirmed* the following: his demeanor and behavior had recently become very negative; he was quite disruptive in the workplace (unintentionally but disruptive nonetheless), speaking loudly on the phone in his open area cubicle; "venting" after calls, and making his way around the office to give others constant updates on his personal struggles; he was doing very little work; and was very distracted (and distracting). As a result, his productivity and that of the team was down. His team members felt badly for him and didn't want to appear unsupportive yet did not know what to do about his disruptive behavior and constant interruptions.

In creating the Remedial Plan, the leader did two things.

First, the leader addressed the How (i.e., the inappropriate conduct/performance) by outlining the concerns regarding his behavior and giving him clear expectations moving forward. Specifically, the employee was told to speak quietly on the phone, end his ongoing "reports" to staff about his personal situation and increase his productivity to acceptable levels. Specific targets were given to him based on his past performance and the general expectations of someone in his position with his level of experience.

Second, the leader addressed the Why (i.e., the personal factors contributing to his performance/behavior issues) by giving the employee specific time in a quiet office to make confidential calls, providing him with a referral to confidential counseling services and granting him permission to leave the office for designated 5-10 minute intervals to "cool down" after particularly stressful or concerning events.

Note that the organization developed its response to this individual's Why (that is, the development of supports for the future) in consultation with and input from him; however, the How (the determination of the specific response to his unacceptable conduct) fell entirely within the purview of the leader.

DETERMINING THE HOW: THE STOVE OF ACCOUNTABILITY

The Stove of Accountability helps leaders determine How to hold individuals accountable for their misconduct or performance issues.

Following an objective review, leaders need to assess where a particular behavior/performance falls on the Scale of Dysfunctional Conduct (see Figure 4, in Chapter 3).

If the individual has no prior disciplinary record and the

conduct/performance falls at 1-2 on the Scale, the leaders should place the individual at Step 1 of the Stove of Accountability and coach the individual using a MIRROR conversation (as outlined above).

Figure 13

THE STOVE OF ACCOUNTABILITY

Step One
Coach:
1. Observation/ concerns
2. Expectations
3. Consequences
4. Follow-through

Step Two
Coach: Same as above; "If ... then ..." consequence changes

Step Three
Internal Office Memorandum Clarifying Expectations (optional step)

Step Four
Letter of Expectation

Step Five
Written Reprimand

Step Six
Minor Suspension

Step Seven
Major Suspension

Step Eight
Termination

If the behavior is closer to 3-4, the leaders may issue the individual a MIRROR letter of expectations.

Anything from 5 on will trigger formal discipline, the severity of which will depend on the seriousness of the investigative findings and conclusions.

If the individual already has a formal disciplinary record, the response to the findings from the most recent review will escalate from his/her last placement on the Stove. Leaders should not begin at Step 1 each time there is newly confirmed dysfunction involving the same individual.

Determining the Why

During investigations, individuals will respond to concerns about their performance or behavior with a list of factors that, in their view, caused or contributed to the circumstances under review. This is their Why.

This information will help inform and guide the development and implementation of supports for the person moving forward. In the example set out above, the employer "heard" the individual's concerns about his marital dispute during the review. While this was not used to justify or excuse his disruptive behavior at the workplace, it was considered and applied in determining how to assist him in the future.

Why-related supports that might be considered in Remedial Plans include (but are certainly not limited to):

- training for the individual;
- education for the team (where others have contributed to the situation);
- adjustment of the person's duties or schedule;
- physical move to a different location in the office/work area;
- transfers to different teams/departments/positions;
- paid or unpaid leaves of absence for personal or family challenges with which an individual is faced;
- medical leaves of absence if there is an underlying condition, such as an illness or addiction, that might be contributing to the behavioral/performance concerns at work; and

- reasonable medical accommodations, developed in accordance with expert medical evidence, for individuals who suffer from a disability that is causing or contributing to the behavioral/performance issues at work.

What if the Remedial Plan Doesn't Remedy the Situation? The Importance of Escalation

There are three critical elements to resolving workplace dysfunction, each of which are critical to the success of the MIRROR Method. We have discussed two at length: respectful *communication* to and about individuals and respectful ongoing *documentation* about that individual.

The third element, and one that is absent in many workplaces, is a clear understanding and consistent application of *measured escalation* in response to *continuing* unacceptable behavior or performance.

MYTH: Leaders should only escalate accountability if the poor behavior or dysfunctional communication worsens.

REALITY: Leaders should escalate accountability if an individual's performance or behavior does not improve after clear expectations and direction have been given to him/her. Leaders should not wait for behavior to become worse – they should escalate if the behavior does not get better.

Instead of measured escalation, employers engage in one of two extremes: over-escalation or non-escalation.

OVER-ESCALATION

At one end of the spectrum, leaders over-escalate and hastily terminate individuals. They jump to Step 8 on the Stove and attempt to justify any relatively serious performance issue or misconduct as a basis to "fire immediately." They fail to give individuals clear notice of their concerns, or a fair opportunity to improve.

Many workplaces who engage in over-escalation end up losing valuable employees who could have been rehabilitated (perhaps in their position or by being placed in an alternate role in the organization). They often end up embroiled in prolonged litigation launched by terminated employees who were caught by surprise, confused about what transpired or angry at not having been heard or given an opportunity to improve. This litigation is costly, both in terms of time and money, regardless of who "wins" at the end of the day.

NON-ESCALATION

At the other end of the spectrum are leaders who fail to escalate at all. Individuals are "coached" (at Step 1 on the Stove) for their entire career, regardless of how serious their misconduct or performance issues have been or how often they have engaged in them. This scenario creates the destructive "bad life" culture of "that's just so-and-so" at 9-10 on the Scale of Dysfunctional Conduct, where individuals learn to accept and expect unacceptable behavior/performance by particular individuals on their team because no one has effectively addressed the situation.

The answer falls between these two extremes, by engaging in *measured escalation*. In brief, this entails the course set out below.

1. As set out above, individuals should be placed on the Stove of Accountability in accordance with the conclusions of the objective review. They should not be automatically placed at Step 1 simply because this is the first time there have been findings against them or concerns about their performance. Their placement on the Stove should be matched with the severity of their dysfunction on the Scale of Dysfunctional Conduct.

2. If someone is already on the Stove and engages in further instances of dysfunctional behavior or performance, the leader should escalate the response, and the individual's accountability, to the next step of the Stove that most accurately reflects the severity of their most recent dysfunction. They should not simply move on to the next step of the Stove.

    For example, if the recent findings are consistent with 7-8 on the Scale of Dysfunctional Conduct, then measured escalation requires a disciplinary response in accordance with this, even if they were only at Step 2 of the Stove previously.

3. If someone is already on the Stove and engages in the *same level* of misconduct, they should be moved to the next step on the Stove. This is because their performance and/or behavior has not improved despite expectations to the contrary. Escalation does not require a worsening of an individual's behavior, only a continuation of it in the face of being directed otherwise.

4. At each step of the Stove, it is important for the leader to be clear and transparent with individuals as to where they are at currently in the non-disciplinary or disciplinary process, how and what they are specifically

expected to change moving forward and the consequences that will flow from their failure to change.

For example, at Step 7 of the Stove, individuals should be advised that if they continue to engage in unacceptable behavior (with specifics as to what that entails), they *will be* terminated (because they will be). There is no reasonable justification for ambiguity, "hints" or "surprises" when it comes to performance management and corrective discipline. This is about an individual's livelihood and – more generally – about an individual's life. Keep this in mind throughout the process.

5. Leaders need to follow through with the consequences that have been communicated to individuals. If, following an objective review, individuals do not improve their behavior/performance in accordance with clearly communicated expectations, then the leader needs to escalate the matter on the Stove.

6. If leaders indicate that they have concerns about specific performance/behavioral issues in the workplace, advise individuals of their expectations for future change, caution individuals about the consequences that will flow should such change not happen, and then fail to follow through with these consequences in the face of continuing issues, leaders will be seen – legally and practically – as condoning the unacceptable behavior through their inaction. This will send mixed messages to the individuals involved and the team in general and will seriously undermine the specific Remedial Plan, the overall MIRROR Method and the day-to-day credibility of the leader involved.

7. If leaders are aware of personal circumstances or mitigating factors in an individual's life that may warrant the absence of escalation in a particular situation, then they should explain this when communicating the Remedial Plan to the employee. For example, if a person is at Level 7 on the Stove, a significant family crisis arises and, during the crisis, that person makes a serious error at work, the leader may not feel comfortable escalating to termination. In these circumstances, the individual should still be held accountable for his/her error by receiving discipline at their pre-existing position on the Stove (Level 7), with an explanation as to why they were not being terminated. This will allow leaders some flexibility with escalation in extenuating/unusual circumstances, provided they explain themselves at the time.

8. Leaders should not suspend escalation on the Stove simply because an individual has protested prior discipline/accountability, through grievances, complaints or other litigation. Leaders need to escalate their actions in response to continuing dysfunction in the workplace; the fact that there are ongoing labor disputes in relation to previous discipline is not a reasonable basis to suspend accountability for ongoing behavior or performance that is unacceptable.

9. Leaders should not suspend escalation, or remove someone from the Stove, because they have left work on a medical or other personal leave. Instead, leaders should "push the pause button" while individuals are on leave and then continue the MIRROR Method process upon their return.

10. Remember that the Stove of Accountability is a tool to use for the How of the Remedial Plan; it does not replace the Why, which takes place through the provision of supports for individuals moving forward.

The ultimate goal of any and all Remedial Plans is to design and implement a comprehensive response, through a combination of accountability, measured escalation and customized supports that will help take and keep the person "off" the Stove altogether.

Step 5

OPERATIONAL RESTORATION: REMEDYING TEAM DYSFUNCTION

tep 5, Operational Restoration, is often not discussed, contemplated or suggested in leadership or legal texts on workplace accountability. It is non-existent in most workplaces. However, it is a key step in the MIRROR Method based on the feedback and recommendations I have received from the many employees with whom I have worked in the course of rebuilding teams after intense drama and dysfunction.

These individuals, whether they were parties, witnesses, bystanders or leaders involved in the dysfunction, all contributed to the insights noted below.

- The longer any workplace dysfunction continues (between individuals, among teams or otherwise), the more complex, toxic and poisonous the overall environment becomes, even if only one or two individuals are directly involved in the dispute.

- As time passes, those directly involved in the dispute become increasingly positional and invested in their "stories" and the "correctness" of their positions. They spend significant amounts of time campaigning to others on their team, in an effort to gain support for their "position."

■ With the passage of time, and the building of camps, parties become less open to compromise, and less willing to solve the problem or rebuild their relationships with others. It eventually becomes more about winning and saving face, not only for themselves, but for the broader group of individuals they have drawn into the dysfunction.

■ During investigations, arbitrations and other formal proceedings, witnesses are summonsed to testify in support of one "side" over the other. This formalizes and further reinforces the informal camps and expands the divide between various individuals on the team.

■ The formal reports/awards that flow from investigations/arbitrations focus on making findings of fact about specific historical events. This often retriggers "old" emotions and reawakens the drama and trauma associated with matters that have long-since passed, which serves to widen the gap even more.

■ The conclusions in these reports/awards often make the workplace environment worse. They create a situation where one "camp" has won and another has lost yet they all must continue to work together.

■ Rarely, if ever, does the "unsuccessful" party read a report/award and say, "Oh, I was wrong." Instead, that party is more likely to conclude that the investigator/adjudicator got it wrong or was manipulated or misled by misinformation provided by the "other side." They maintain their perspective and position on the issue, with perhaps even more vehemence than before, along with anger and resentment over how the process unfolded. No award, no matter how well written or thoroughly analyzed, will persuade someone out of his/her personal perspective or emotional experience regarding what happened.

■ These reports/awards rarely contain recommendations on how to solve the broader or continuing dysfunction in the workplace. This is because investigators, arbitrators and adjudicators often lack the necessary jurisdiction to solve the underlying problem. Their mandate is restricted to making findings and drawing conclusions about narrowly defined disputes that occurred in the past.

■ Following implementation of the award/report, parties, bystanders, leaders and witnesses return to the worksite. The file is closed and everyone is expected to resume their normal day-to-day interactions with each other. This does not happen.

■ Team breakdowns of this nature arise in many different situations, not only those involving litigation. For example, systemic dysfunction may arise in the face of significant operational change, lay-offs and associated rights to "bump" others out of their positions, medical leaves, returns to work and specific accommodations for particular employees. Most commonly, the dysfunction related to these issues stems from the lack of timely or transparent communication surrounding these situations.

■ At an even more basic level, teams will break down – even in the absence of formal litigation or significant operational change – in the face of any continuing disruption or dysfunction, by employees or leaders, that is allowed to continue over a prolonged period of time.

Operational Restoration: What Does it Look Like?

In intense, emotional and adversarial situations, individuals, dyads and/or entire teams cannot magically move forward in the face of residual negative feelings and dynamics unless they are provided with a Restorative process to debrief, obtain closure (at least at the workplace) *and* take steps to gradually rebuild trust and communication among the team. In the same way that Dots of dysfunction take time to turn into train wrecks, it takes time to transform train wrecks into healthy and productive teams. Operational Restoration is an excellent first step in this process of rebuilding.

Whether it is necessary to implement Operational Restoration in any given situation will depend on the circumstances involved.

If the MIRROR Method was implemented in response to an individual's performance or behavioral issues that had little involvement of or effect on other individuals or the team, then the situation might be addressed sufficiently through an individualized Remedial Plan.

If, during the course of the MIRROR Method, it becomes apparent that, in addition to there being issues with an individual's behavior/performance (which will be addressed through the individualized Remedial Plan), there is ongoing dysfunction between individuals (which often affects others on the team), the Operational Restoration might consist of a confidential mandatory mediation between them. This mediation may involve a leader with an employee, or two employees on their own.

This route would allow both individuals an opportunity to debrief about what transpired in the past (in a safe and respectful manner) and then work on practical steps to which each will commit, moving forward, in an effort to rebuild a manageable working relationship. This plan does not require them to be friends; it simply requires them to agree to take practical actions to ensure they relate with each other with civility and respect.

If, during the course of the MIRROR Method, it becomes apparent that the team has been fractured by prolonged dysfunction by an individual or between individuals, then leaders should facilitate a team-building session, similar to the mediation set out above, for those involved in:

- the initial dysfunction (either as a party, bystander or witness);

- the subsequent fall-out (by being drawn into camps, cliques, gossip or otherwise); or

- the formal investigative or adjudicative process.

As with mediation between two individuals, this process should be twofold in nature.

1. First, every individual on the team should be allowed to debrief about their experience in or with the past dysfunction and its effect on their current work environment, in a manner that protects the confidentiality of those directly involved and any related processes/ Remedial Plans that have been implemented.

2. Following a structured and safe debriefing process, the team should work together to build a specific and practical framework on how they plan to move forward and work together in rebuilding trust and communication with each other (based on their knowledge, from

their past experiences, as to what has worked and what hasn't).

MYTH: Leaders should not arrange a team-building session or restorative process for the group because it will violate individual rights to confidentiality.

REALITY: Often, everyone including those directly involved in a workplace situation would welcome an opportunity to discuss what happened so they can move forward on new footing. The objective of a team-building process is to discuss how the team will work together in the future rather than focus on the past. Specific confidential issues do not need to be disclosed during this process (although on many occasions, individuals directly involved choose to self-disclose or consent to such disclosure as a constructive step towards closure).

The leadership team should be active participants in and not facilitators of this process. This needs to be conducted by someone external to the department, with significant experience in working with complex team building and Restoration of workplace practices regarding respectful communication and conduct.

The Importance of Closure

Following this Operational Restoration, individuals should be expected to let go of what transpired in the past in terms of both the dysfunction that happened and the processes employed to resolve it. Consistent with this, there should be no further discussion about these matters at the workplace.

No one is expected to agree with the outcome of a formal investigation or Restorative process. They must, however, accept that "it is what it is." The formal investigation/process is over and a general communication and behavioral framework has been agreed to by the team as a whole. As a member of the team, they must make all reasonable efforts to engage and communicate with others – moving forward – in a respectful and civil manner.

If individuals fail to respect the expectation of closure, and continue to breed negativity, cynicism and division at the workplace through ongoing discussions about the past, their behavior and attitude will constitute Dots that need to be addressed through the MIRROR Method. If individuals are not held accountable for this type of behavior, the minority of staff who refuse to let go of these issues will burn out the majority of staff who have let it go and wish to move on and build a respectful and productive team.

Step 6

REVISITING THE SCENE OF THE DYSFUNCTION

The final step in the MIRROR Method requires leaders to return to the scene of the former dysfunction to determine if the Remedial Plans and Operational Restoration have, in fact, remedied the situation.

The expression "let sleeping dogs lie" has no place in the workplace, particularly in circumstances regarding workplace dysfunction. This is akin to letting a Dot fester into a train wreck, by turning a blind eye to the possibility of concerns. As we have explored earlier in this book, this is exactly what a leader should not do.

When designing Remedial Plans, leaders use their best informed judgment, based on the results of the Review and ongoing discussions with individuals involved, to solve the problem. They are hopeful that the combination of accountability and supports will facilitate the necessary and expected changes in an individual's behavior/performance and the Operational Restorative processes will rebuild civility and respect for the team as a whole.

However, this does not always happen. Leaders can do their best to influence a positive outcome but, ultimately, they do not have control over the decisions and behaviors of others.

In order to assess the success of the Remedial Plans and the Operational Restorative processes, it is important for leaders to monitor the workplace (as they are expected to do in any event) to determine whether or not the situation involving past dysfunction has been resolved.

If they observe or hear about concerns, leaders should initiate the MIRROR Method again, and this time, escalate accountability (should the concerns be verified through an objective review). They also should Revisit the supports they had implemented previously to determine whether additional or different supports should be added or replaced.

Even if leaders do not observe or hear about concerns, they should return to the scene 3 months after the process concluded (or earlier in circumstances of significant dysfunction) to specifically inquire into the situation to determine whether it has improved to an acceptable level.

During this check-in, leaders should perform the tasks outlined below.

1. Ensure the supports, such as training, counseling or medical accommodations, were implemented as agreed or directed. Often, during this check-in, leaders become aware of individuals who have failed to complete training, comply with required treatment programs or complete particular qualifications. This stage allows "missed" steps to be detected and provides an opportunity to put the Remedial Plan back on track.

2. Assess whether the supports (in combination with prior accountability) successfully resolved the workplace dysfunction. This is determined by confidentially checking in with those involved to ascertain whether or not the concerning behavior/performance continued following completion of the MIRROR Method.

3. If, during the course of this assessment, the leader determines that the concerns have continued (or new ones have appeared), the MIRROR Method needs to be initiated.

MYTH: For the sake of closure, it is important not to discuss issues after an investigation has been completed and remedies have been implemented. At that point, leaders should operate on the premise that "no news is good news."

REALITY: Workplace dysfunction is a dynamic, not a specific incident or event. Remedial Plans are "educated best guesses" into what will work to address this dysfunction. In order to ensure such plans are, indeed, successful in resolving the dysfunction, leaders need to check in with those involved after a period of time has elapsed.

Revisiting the scene of the (former) dysfunction is a specialized and necessary form of monitoring that, if done effectively and consistently, will ensure that Remedial Plans either work in *substance* or are *re-worked* in practice.

The elimination of workplace dysfunction is too important to the health and productivity of individuals and teams to simply leave to chance. A genuine and comprehensive approach to the ending of workplace drama and dysfunction requires that leaders proactively check in with those involved, after the fact, to ensure the dysfunction has been adequately addressed. If it hasn't been, then the MIRROR Method needs to begin again.

The Ending of the Book And the Beginning of a New Workplace

Despite numerous leadership "pitches" out there, there is no quick fix or panacea to the elimination of workplace dysfunction. There is no magical leadership style or one-size-fits-all leadership theory that, if followed diligently, will guarantee the eradication of all performance and behavioral concerns in the workplace. Simply put, there is no magic wand.

That said, the MIRROR Method is the next best thing to a magic wand. It provides leaders, at all levels of any organization, small or large, unionized or not, with a straightforward procedural framework to follow in order to best manage workplace dysfunction.

If the MIRROR Method is applied consistently and respectfully, leaders will be able to demonstrate that they did all they could to detect dysfunction early, diagnose dysfunction objectively and deal with dysfunction fairly, implementing a comprehensive and balanced Remedial Plan.

Ultimately, leaders cannot know, with certainty, whether their leadership decisions will be upheld by third-party adjudicators or result in necessary positive change in their staff. However, with proper use and application of the MIRROR Method, they can be sure that the processes they use to *arrive* at and *implement* those decisions will be accepted as respectful, objective and fair. This is all that leaders, and those who rely on their ongoing expertise and support, should expect.

One final note: please remember that it truly is *all about the How*. At the end of the day, whether or not particular decisions are upheld or overturned, what is fundamental to the creation of respectful workplaces, the implementation of the MIRROR Method and the integrity of leaders everywhere is *how* they respond to workplace dysfunction. If leaders treat their teams with basic civility and respect and demand the same in others, they are walking the talk of true respect in the workplace. There is no training more powerful than watching leaders show us how it's done.

Frequently Asked Questions

I have been training leaders on how to build respectful and productive teams for many years. Throughout the course of these sessions, I have received a number of similar questions from many different organizations, regardless of the size of company or type of industry involved.

I have included brief answers to some of these questions below. These answers should be read within the broader context of the MIRROR Method in its entirety.

What do we do about individuals who have been "challenging" to a workplace for a long time but have never been addressed?

These individuals have to be "managed" in the same way as others, using the MIRROR Method. However, given the long-standing nature of the issues, the initial investigation for these individuals often will be more formal than for those who are, in fact, involved in dysfunction for the first time. The remedy will be based on the findings and conclusions of the objective investigation, not the longstanding history leading up to it.

The employee cannot be placed at 8 on the Stove of Accountability, and issued significant discipline, simply because he/she has caused dysfunction for many years. However, he/she *may* be placed at an 8 if the seriousness of the issues, as confirmed by the investigation, warrants it.

What if a new leader has inherited an old problem (in terms of dysfunctional behavior of individuals or teams)?

See above. The new leader has an obligation to initiate the MIRROR Method, even if previous leaders failed to inquire into or address the same dysfunction. Employees may accuse the new leader of "targeting" them, based on the history of inaction by others, but in the absence of any disrespectful conduct on the part of the leader, there is no reasonable basis to this challenge. Further, fear of this type of challenge is not a reasonable basis for continuing inaction on the part of leadership.

What if the leader is the one with the issue?

If the leader has caused or contributed to the dysfunction, then their behavior needs to be objectively reviewed and remedied by senior management/the executive team, using the MIRROR Method.

What if the leader is friends, or works closely, with either the complainant or the one accused of engaging in dysfunctional behavior or conduct?

Perceptions of preferential treatment, real or imagined, cause significant credibility issues for leaders. The results of the MIRROR Method will not be seen or accepted as credible if the leader involved is seen to be friends with one of the parties involved. Leaders need to remain at arm's length from their team.

If leaders find themselves in a position of being friends with, or being seen as being close with, a particular staff member, they should not be involved in the MIRROR Method process (or any other decisions involving that person's hiring, discipline or accountability).

What if the person "manages up?"

A number of individuals engage in dysfunctional conduct toward some or all of their peers or subordinates yet demonstrate the utmost respect and civility towards leaders within and outside the organization. For this reason, leaders should not prejudge complaints or concerns that come forward based on their own experience with the individual (i.e. "that can't be true – they are *never* like that with me!").

Instead, they should inquire into and assess the concern objectively, through strict adherence to the MIRROR Method. If they find that they are unable to be objective (or appear objective), they should step away from the process and have someone who is more distant to the individual facilitate the MIRROR Method process.

What if the individual has a disability that is causing the behavioral/performance issues?

This issue is one of many that would need to be investigated through the MIRROR Method. If an individual raises a disability at any time during the review, the leader should objectively inquire into this assertion by obtaining necessary objective medical evidence to:

1. confirm or rule out the asserted disability;

2. better understand the nature of the disability and how it manifests in the workplace;

3. determine if and how it caused or contributed to the alleged performance/behavioral concerns; and

4. determine whether it can be reasonably accommodated so that the person is able to perform and behave at an acceptable and safe standard moving forward.

What if the organization doesn't take action against the person because "that's just the way they are?"

A respectful and productive workplace will only be sustainable if the organization commits to holding everyone accountable for dysfunctional and disrespectful conduct. Individuals are "just the way they are" because organizations have allowed them to remain that way.

Organizations need to develop institutional courage and consistency to ensure that all Dots of dysfunction, regardless of the person's position, history or influence within the organization, are properly evaluated and addressed through the MIRROR Method.

What if the person is a "star" and the CEO doesn't want him/her to leave?

First, individuals are never "stars," regardless of their metrics, sales, productivity, industry connections or otherwise, if their behavior/performance creates disruption, damage and destruction to other individuals or the team in general. They may be valuable contributors to the organization and there may be significant interest in retaining them, but they are not "stars." They are individuals with both strengths and weaknesses, each of which need to be recognized by the leader.

Second, addressing someone's dysfunctional conduct does not mean they should be forced to leave the organization. It simply requires them to be accountable for their conduct and communication and treat others with basic civility and respect. If they refuse to do so, the organization has to consider the resulting costs to other members of the team (who also are valuable contributors) and the costs to the overall organization (through loss of reputation, litigation, turnover and otherwise) should it continue to prefer the personal interests and preferences of one individual over the rights of others.

What if someone breaches confidentiality or retaliates against others during a review?

Workplace reviews are expected to be confidential processes. Parties and witnesses should not be discussing anything associated with the investigation with anyone. Those conducting the review should disclose information on a need-to-know basis only.

Further no one involved in an investigation may retaliate against others, indirectly or directly, and should not attempt to influence the outcome of the investigation in any way.

An alleged failure to comply with either of these expectations, by anyone, should be considered Dots that need to be reviewed and addressed through the MIRROR Method.

Do you need advice on how to move forward with a specific individual or team?

Are you interested in providing your leadership team with helpful strategies and practical training on the MIRROR Method?

Would you like Marli to speak at an upcoming workplace event or industry conference?

In addition to being an author, investigator and arbitrator, Marli is a highly engaging, experienced and well-known workplace consultant, educator and keynote speaker.

Book Marli now at
www.marlirusen.com

Watch for Marli's next book,
WALKING ON EGGSHELLS,
which will offer practical strategies on
addressing workplace dysfunction –
for every member of the team.